A Scientist's Equipment

Scientists use many different kinds of special equipment in a laboratory.

Label each piece of equipment.

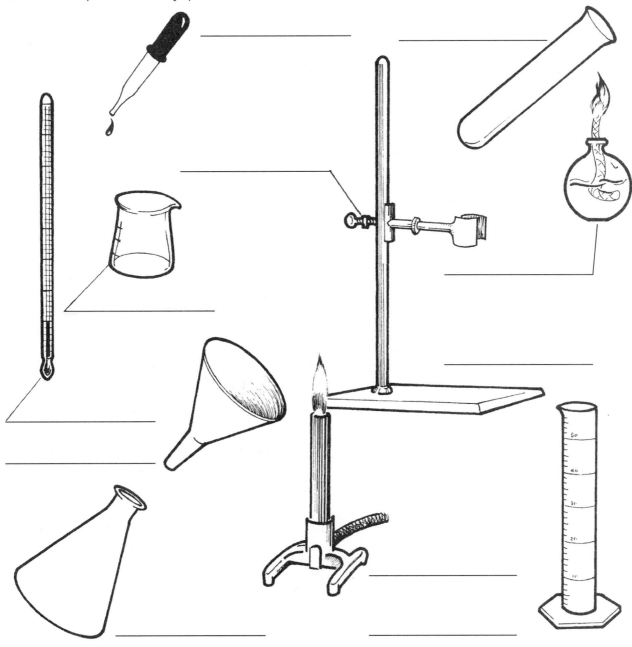

alcohol lamp	flask	test tube
beaker	funnel	test tube clamp
Bunsen burner	graduated cylinder	thermometer
dropper	ring stand	

How Long Is It?

The **meter** is the standard unit of measurement when measuring the length of an object or the distance between two objects.

Use *kilometer, meter, centimeter,* or *millimeter* to label the unit used to measure each object.

The Long and Short of It

Weight, length, area, and volume are properties of matter that scientists can measure. Scientists use the units of grams, meters, and liters to measure these properties.

Write the abbreviation for each unit of measurement.

Unit of Measure	Abbreviation
gram	
kilogram	
milligram	
meter	
kilometer	
centimeter	
millimeter	
square centimeters	
cubic centimeters	
liter	
milliliter	

cm	kg	mg
cm²	km	mL
cm³	L	mm
g	m	

Balances

The mass of an <u>object</u> can be measured using a balance. Two common types of balances are the **triple beam balance** and the **double pan balance**.

Name each balance and label the parts. The words in the word bank may be used more than once.

Balance: _____

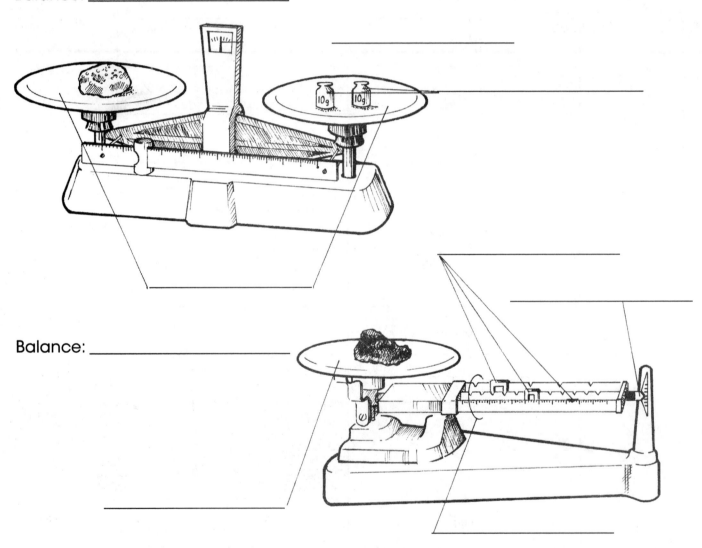

Balance: _____

beams	mass	pans	riders
double pan balance	pan	pointer	triple beam balance

Reading a Double Pan Balance

To determine the weight of an object using a double pan balance, find the <u>sum of</u> <u>masses needed to balance the two pans</u>. Do this by making the pointer on the balance <u>line up</u> with the indicated line.

Find the mass of each object.

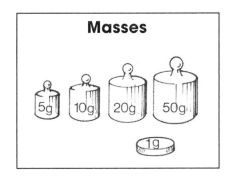

1. _____ g

2. _____ g

3. _____ g

4. _____ g

Name_____

Reading a Triple Beam Balance

To determine the mass or weight of an object using a triple beam balance, find the sum of the masses shown on the riders.

Find the mass indicated on each triple beam balance.

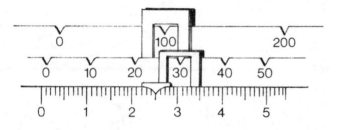

1. _____

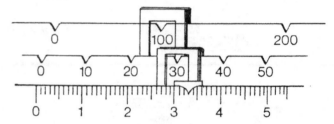

4. _____

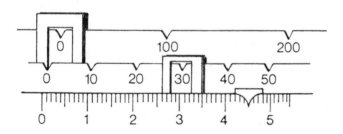

2. _____

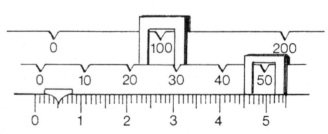

5. _____

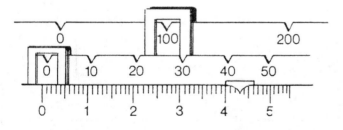

3. _____

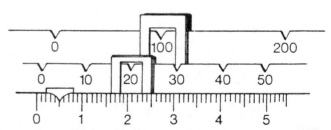

6. _____

Celsius vs. Fahrenheit

The thermometer compares the Celsius and Fahrenheit scales. Label the temperatures on the Celsius and Fahrenheit scales.

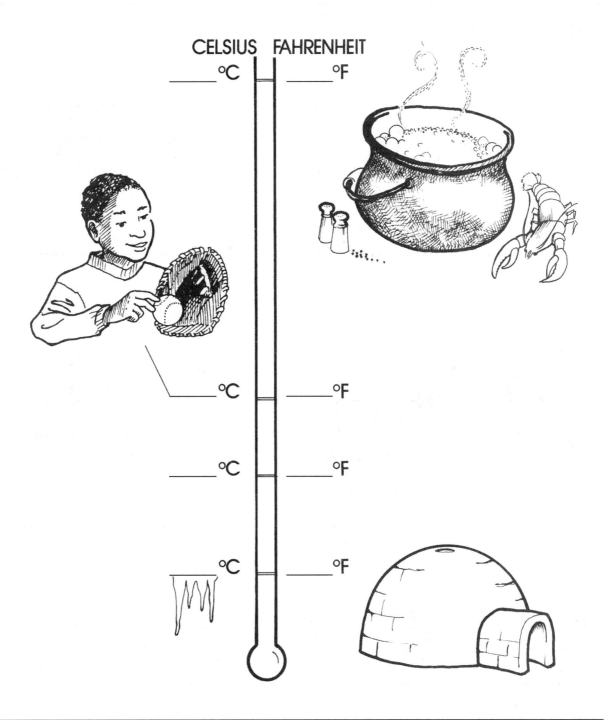

0	32	68	100
20	37	98.6	212

Reading a Graduated Cylinder

Small quantities of a liquid can be measured using a graduated cylinder. Notice how the liquid curves up the side of the cylinder. To get an accurate reading, read the measurement at the bottom of the curve, or **meniscus**.

Read and record each volume.

1. _____ mL

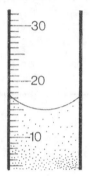

5. _____ mL

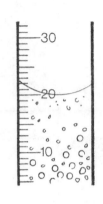

2. _____ mL

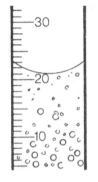

6. _____ mL

3. _____ mL

7. _____ mL

4. _____ mL

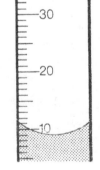

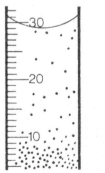

8. _____ mL

Periodic Table of the Elements

The **periodic table** gives a lot of information about each element.

Label the information that the words, numbers, and letters represent for each element.

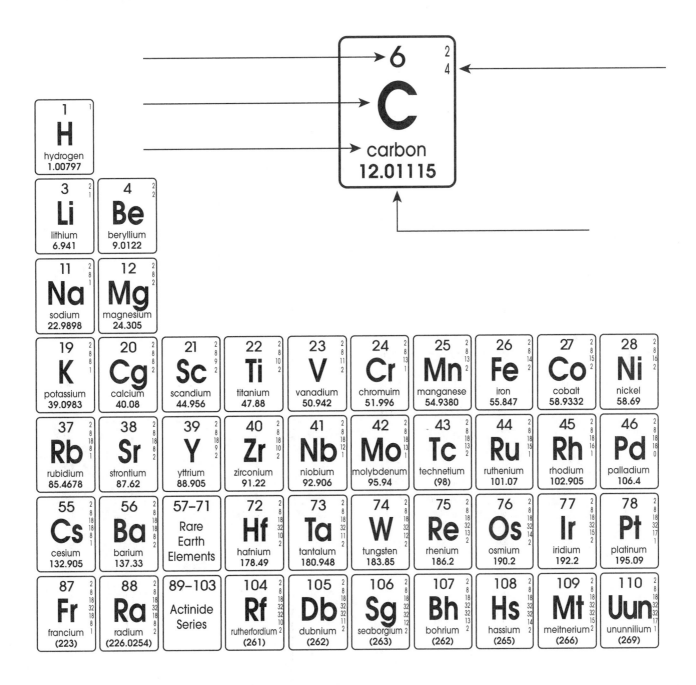

atomic mass	electrons in outer shell	element's symbol
atomic number	element's name	

Chemical Symbols Crossword

Complete the crossword puzzle by matching the symbols to the names of the elements.

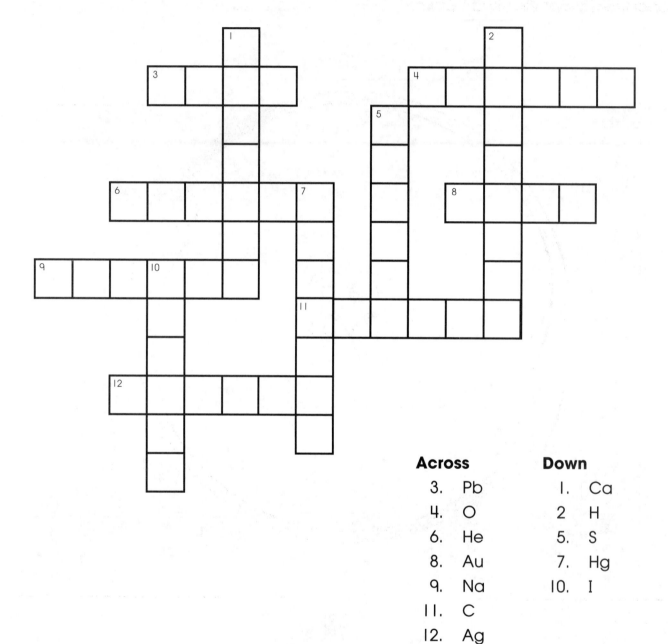

Across
3. Pb
4. O
6. He
8. Au
9. Na
11. C
12. Ag

Down
1. Ca
2 H
5. S
7. Hg
10. I

calcium	helium	lead	silver
carbon	hydrogen	mercury	sodium
gold	iodine	oxygen	sulfur

Atoms

All elements are made up of atoms. The **atom** is the smallest particle of an element.

Label the parts of the helium atom.

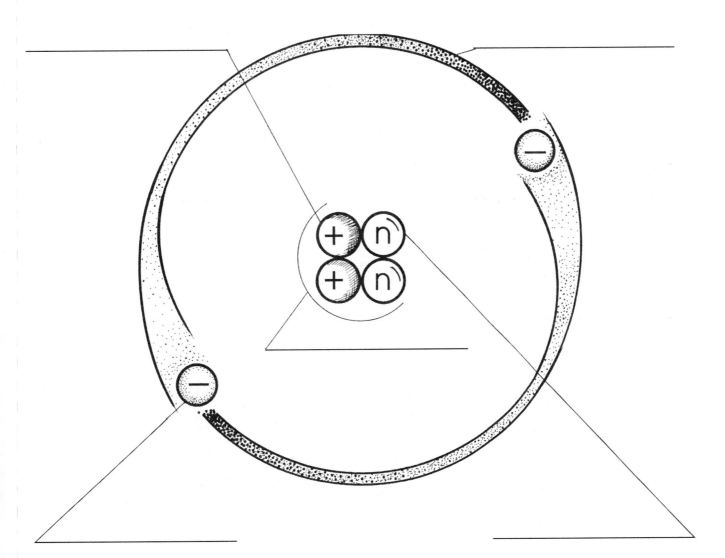

| electron | nucleus | proton |
| neutron | orbit (shell) | |

Protons, Neutrons, and Electrons

The **atomic number** of an atom is the number of protons in each atom of that element. Because atoms are electrically neutral, the atomic number is also the number of electrons. The **atomic mass** tells the number of protons and neutrons in an atom. By subtracting the atomic number from the atomic mass, you can find the number of neutrons.

Complete the chart. Round atomic numbers to the nearest whole number.

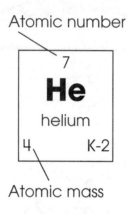

Atomic number

He
helium

4   K-2

Atomic mass

Helium Atom

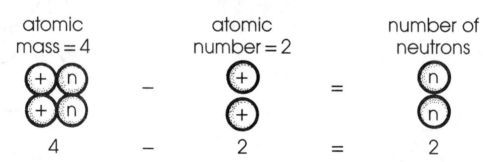

atomic mass = 4		atomic number = 2		number of neutrons
4	−	2	=	2

Element	Symbol	Atomic Number	Atomic Mass	Protons	Neutrons	Electrons
helium	He	2	4			
nitrogen	N	7	14			7
carbon	C	6	12			
sodium	Na	11	23			
iron	Fe	26			30	
copper	Cu		64	29		
silver	Ag	47	108		61	

Name That Molecule!

Write the chemical formula for each molecule.

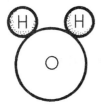

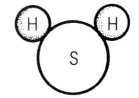

_____

_____

_____

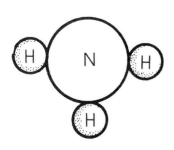

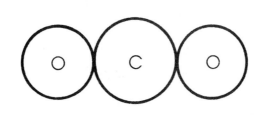

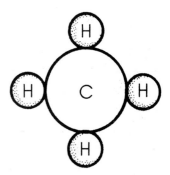

_____

_____

_____

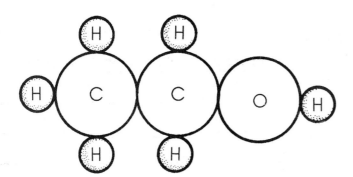

_____

CH_4	CO_2	H_2O	NH_3
C_2H_5OH	Fe_2O_3	H_2S	

Chemical Formulas

A **chemical formula** is a shorthand way to write the name of a compound.

Complete the chart for each formula. Some words may be used more than once.

	Compound	Formula	Elements
1.		NaCl	
2.		HCl	
3.		NaOH	
4.		H_2O	
5.		CO_2	
6.		H_2SO_4	
7.		$CuSO_4$	
8.		C_2H_5OH	

alcohol	copper	oxygen	sulfur
carbon	copper sulfate	sodium	sulfuric acid
carbon dioxide	hydrochloric acid	sodium chloride	water
chlorine	hydrogen	sodium hydroxide	

Name_____

Chemicals Crossword

Use what you have learned about chemicals to complete the puzzle. You may refer to your science book, an encyclopedia, or the Internet.

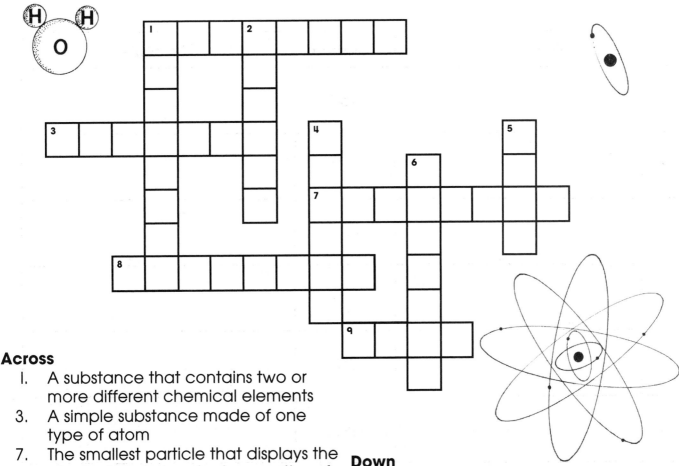

Across

1. A substance that contains two or more different chemical elements
3. A simple substance made of one type of atom
7. The smallest particle that displays the physical and chemical properties of a compound
8. A negatively charged particle that orbits the nucleus of an atom
9. What everything is made of; the smallest unit of an element

Down

1. Any substance obtained by or used in a chemical process
2. A positively charged particle found free or in a nucleus
4. It stands for the name of an element.
5. *Au* is the symbol for ____.
6. A particle in an atom or by itself with no electrical charge

atom	compound	gold	proton
chemical	electron	molecule	symbol
	element	neutron	

Dry Cells

The **dry cell** is a source of portable power used in flashlights, toys, and radios.
Three basic kinds of dry cells are commonly used—carbon-zinc, alkaline, and mercury.

Label the parts of the carbon-zinc dry cell.

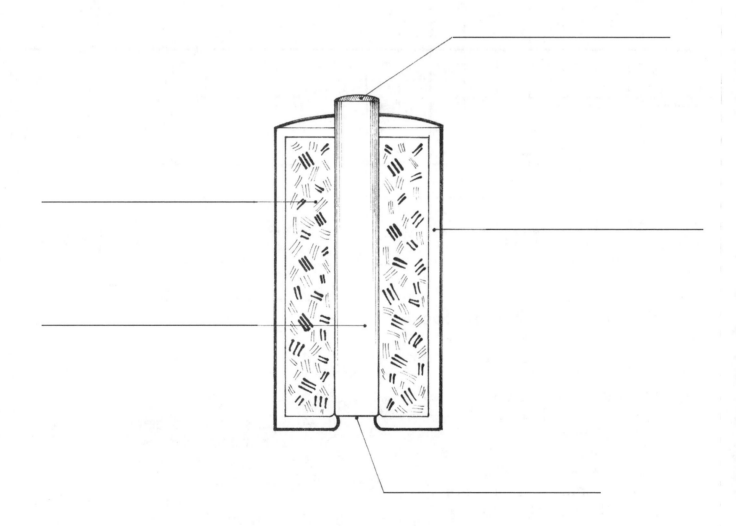

carbon rod	negative terminal	zinc container
chemical paste	positive terminal	

Lightbulbs

Label the parts of the incandescent lightbulb.

base	connecting and	contact	glass support
bulb	supporting wires	filaments	

Circuits and Switches

To be useful, electricity must flow in a circuit. Electric circuits can be illustrated with the help of symbols.

Identify each symbol.

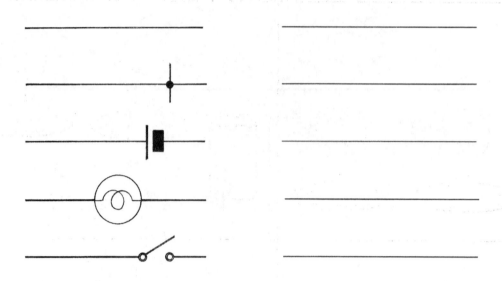

Name each circuit.

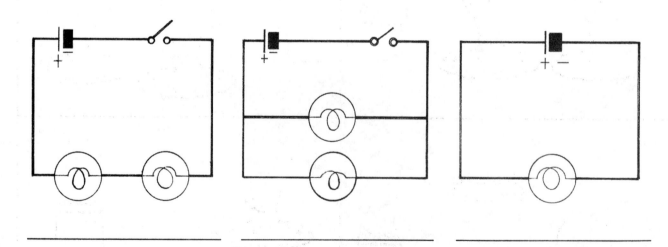

_____   _____   _____

battery	lightbulb	series circuit	switch
connection	parallel circuit	simple circuit	wire

Drawing Electrical Circuits

There are three types of simple electrical circuits: a **closed circuit**, a **parallel circuit**, and a **series circuit**. Each type can be set up in more than one way.

Draw lines to show where the wires should connect to make each circuit.

Classy Levers

Three classes of levers exist. Levers are identified by the position of the fulcrum and the <u>load.</u>

Label each class of lever and the three lever parts. Some words will be used more than once.

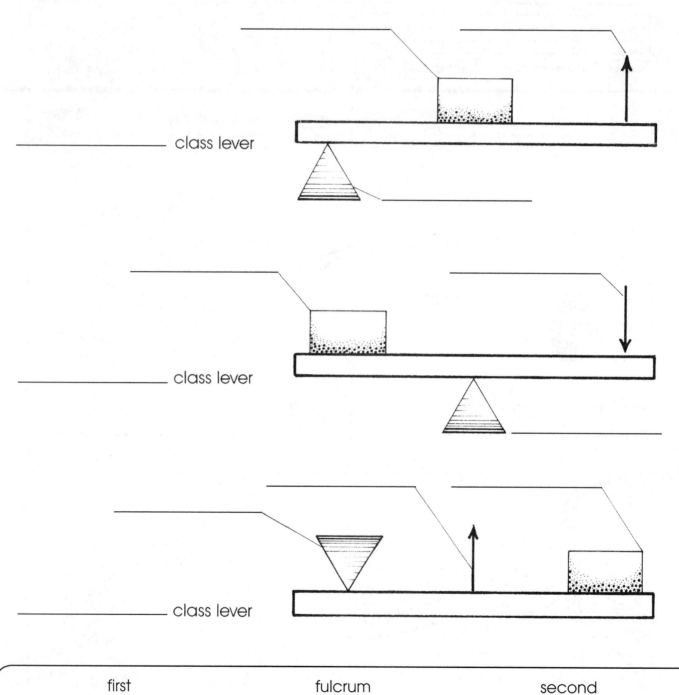

_____ class lever

_____ class lever

_____ class lever

first	fulcrum	second
force	load	third

Name_____

Practical Levers

Under each object, identify the class of the lever as *first*, *second*, or *third*.

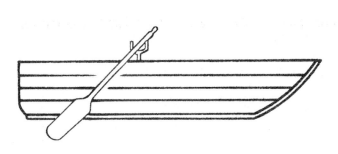

_____

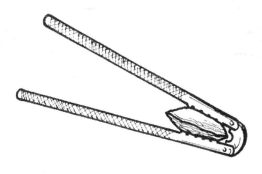

_____

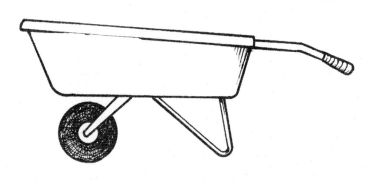

_____

_____

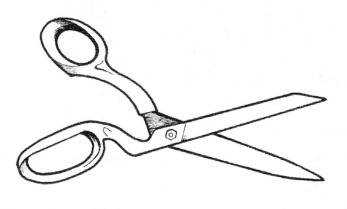

_____

_____

Special Inclined Planes

Some simple machines are special inclined planes, called wedges and screws. A wedge is an inclined plane that exerts force to widen a space. In a screw, the inclined plane is wrapped around a central point.

Place an **X** on the simple machines that are not special inclined planes. Label the special inclined planes either *screw* or *wedge.*

Pedal Power

Most machines use a combination of simple machines to work. For example, your bicycle is a combination of many simple machines. Study the bicycle on this page.

Circle and label as many simple machines as you can find on the bicycle.

| inclined plane (screw) | lever | wheel and axle |

Compound Machines

Often <u>two or more simple machines are combined to make one machine</u> called a **compound machine**.

Name the simple machines that are combined to make each compound machine.

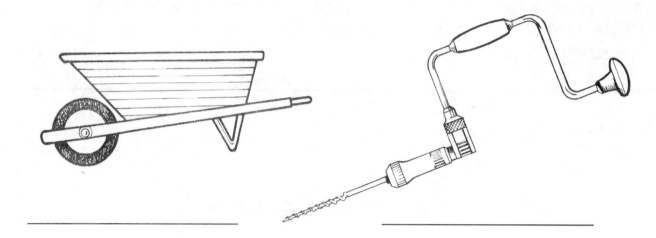

_____   _____

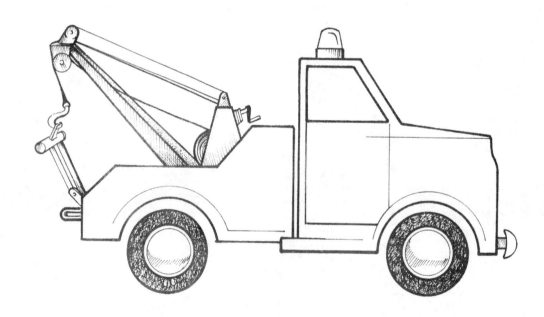

_____

inclined plane (wedge, screw)	lever	wheel and axle
	pulley	

The Seasons

Seasons are important events in Earth's yearly weather cycle. The diagram shows Earth's position in its orbit on four different dates. The seasons are a result of Earth's position in its orbit. Two solstices and two equinoxes occur each year around the same time, though the actual date may vary by a few days.

On the solid lines, label the approximate equinox and solstice dates. On the dotted lines, name the season for the Northern Hemisphere.

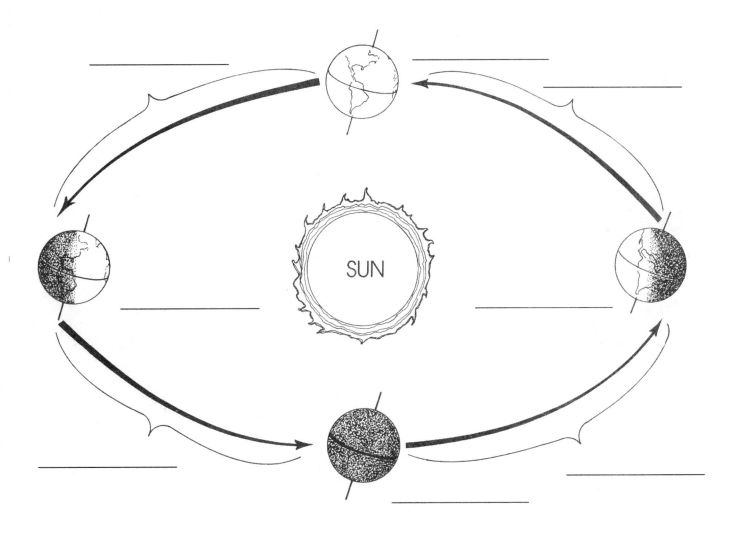

| autumn | June 21 | September 22 | summer |
| December 22 | March 20 | spring | winter |

Summer and Winter

The illustration shows Earth's position in relation to the sun for summer and winter in the Northern Hemisphere.

Label the seasons for the Northern Hemisphere, and name the imaginary lines of latitude on Earth.

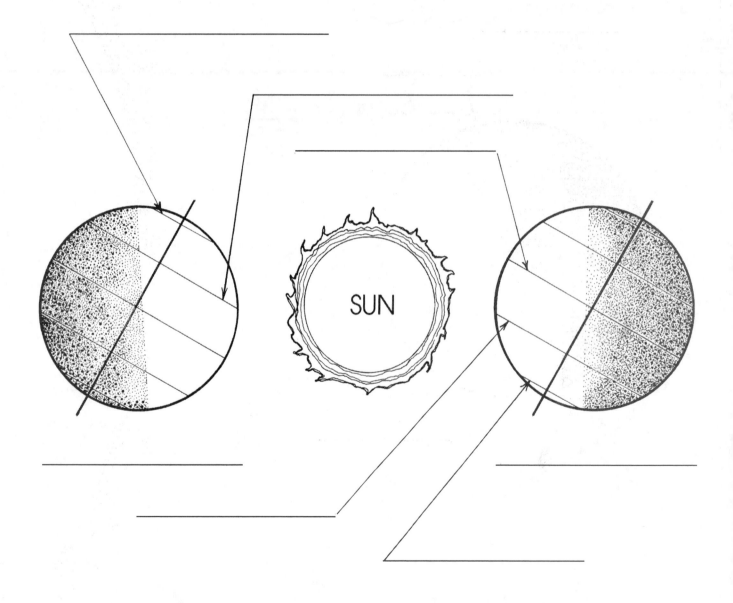

SUN

_____   _____

_____

| Antarctic Circle | equator | Tropic of Cancer | winter |
| Arctic Circle | summer | Tropic of Capricorn | |

Day and Night

Day and night are the result of Earth's rotation on its axis.

Label the diagram.

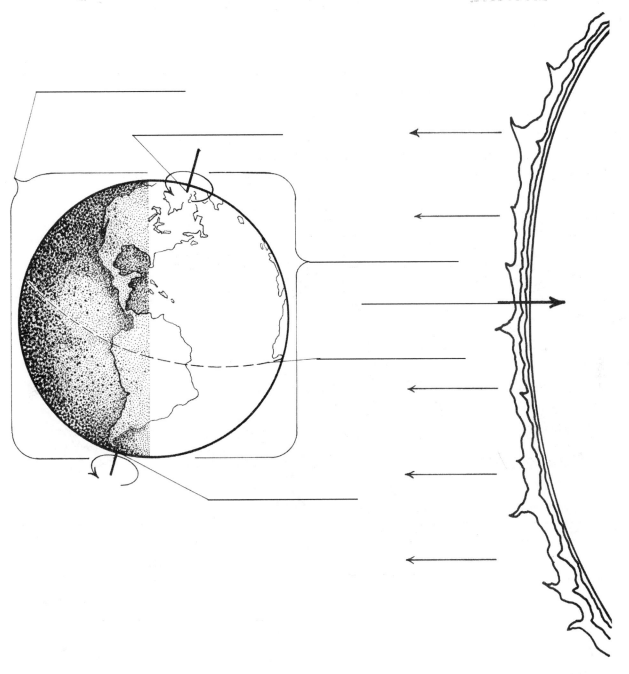

day	night	South Pole
equator	North Pole	sun

High Tide

The ocean tides are the result of gravitational forces from the sun, moon, and rotation of our Earth. When the sun, moon, and Earth line up, the gravitational pull is greatest, causing the highest tides, the **spring tides**. The lowest tides, **neap tides**, occur when the sun, Earth, and moon form right angles.

Label each diagram.

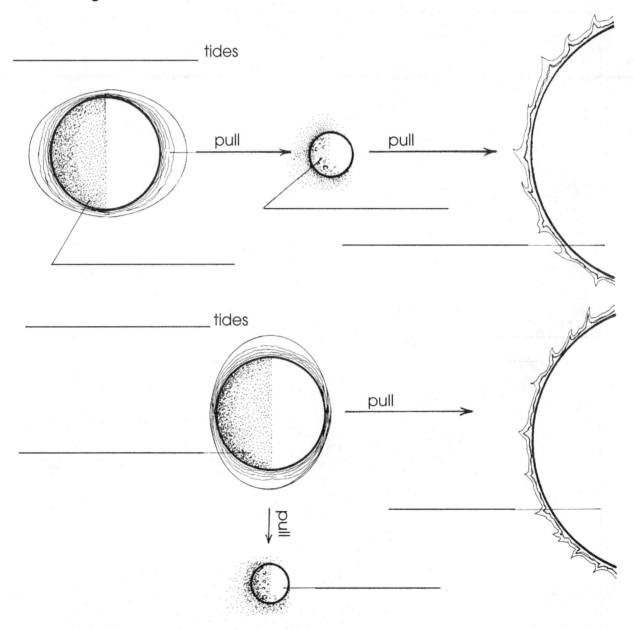

_____ tides

pull   pull

_____ tides

pull

pull

Earth	neap	sun
moon	spring	

Space Shadows

When the sun, moon, and Earth are in the proper alignment, either the moon can cast a shadow on Earth, or Earth can cast a shadow on the moon. This is known as an **eclipse**.

Draw the position of the moon and the shadows for both a lunar and solar eclipse. Label the type of eclipse.

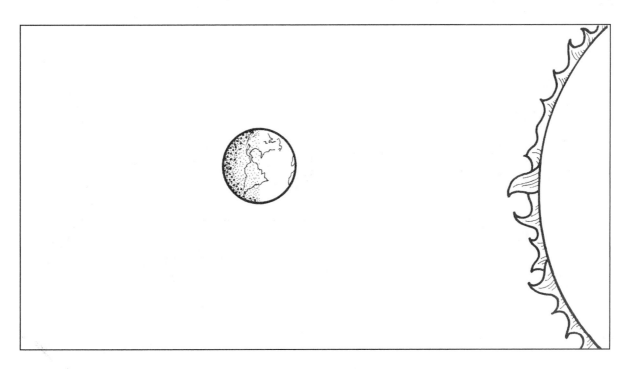

Earth's Shadow

When the sun, Earth, and moon are in a direct line, the moon moves into Earth's shadow, causing a **lunar eclipse**.

Label the orbits and bodies in the diagram.

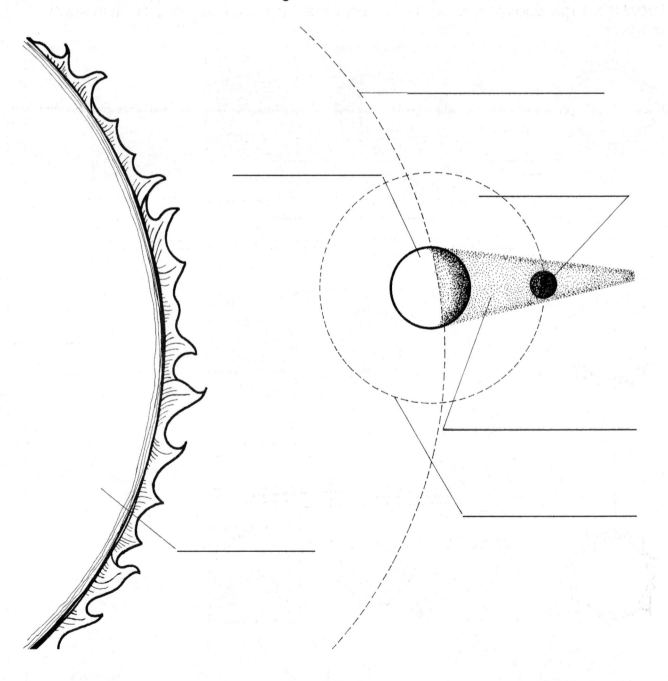

| Earth | Earth's shadow | moon's orbit |
| Earth's orbit | moon | sun |

Moon Shadows

When the new moon is directly between Earth and the sun, an eclipse of the sun occurs. The type of **solar eclipse** that occurs depends on how much sunlight the moon blocks from the view on Earth.

Label the three kinds of solar eclipse. Then, label the moon, sun, and Earth in each diagram.

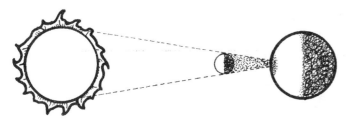 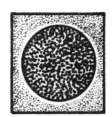   _____

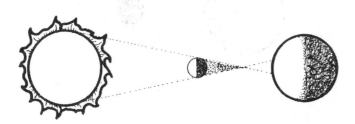    _____

    _____

annular eclipse	moon	sun
Earth	partial eclipse	total eclipse

Changing Faces

As the moon revolves around Earth, we can see different amounts of the moon's lighted side. Study the diagram of the moon's different phases and each phase as it would be seen from Earth.

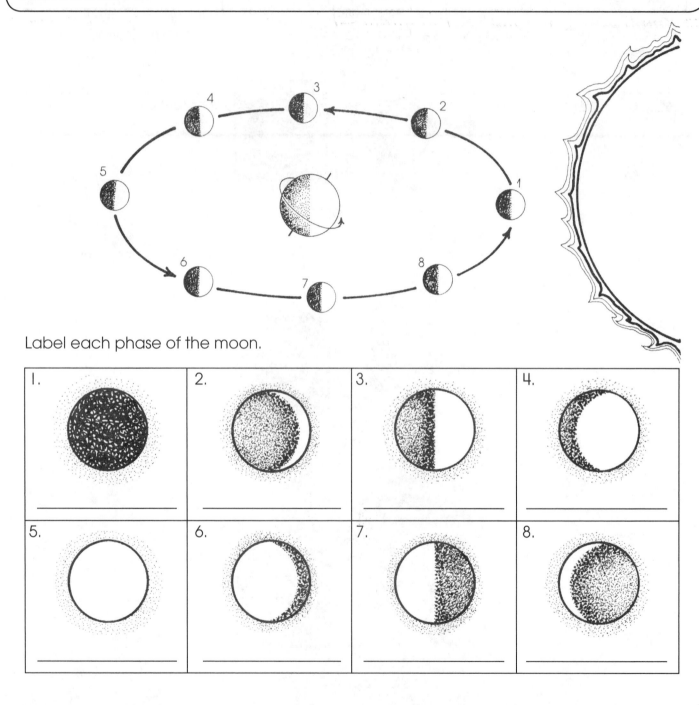

Label each phase of the moon.

1.	2.	3.	4.
_____	_____	_____	_____

5.	6.	7.	8.
_____	_____	_____	_____

first quarter	last quarter	waning crescent	waxing crescent
full moon	new moon	waning gibbous	waxing gibbous

Waning and Waxing Moon

Label the different phases of the moon.

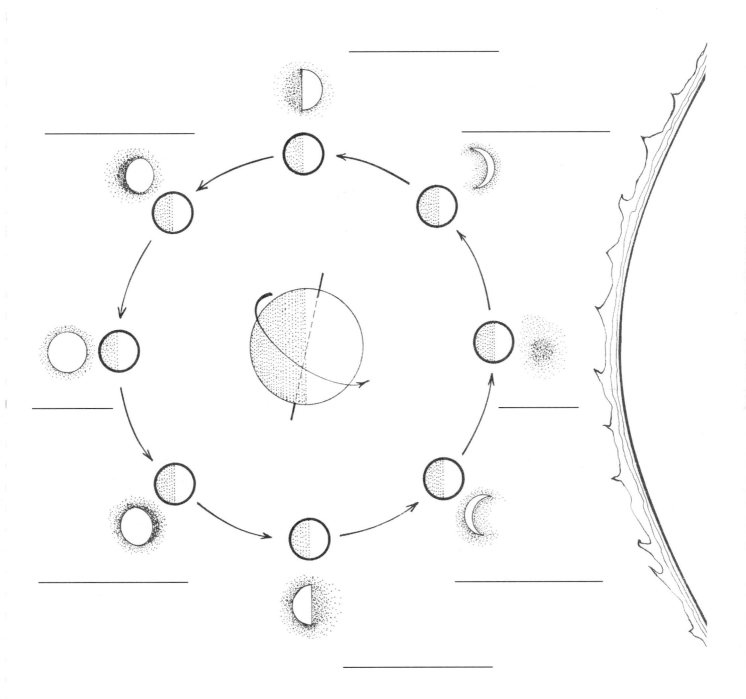

| first quarter | last quarter | waning crescent | waxing crescent |
| full moon | new moon | waning gibbous | waxing gibbous |

Planets of the Solar System

All of the planets of the solar system travel around the sun.

Label the planets.

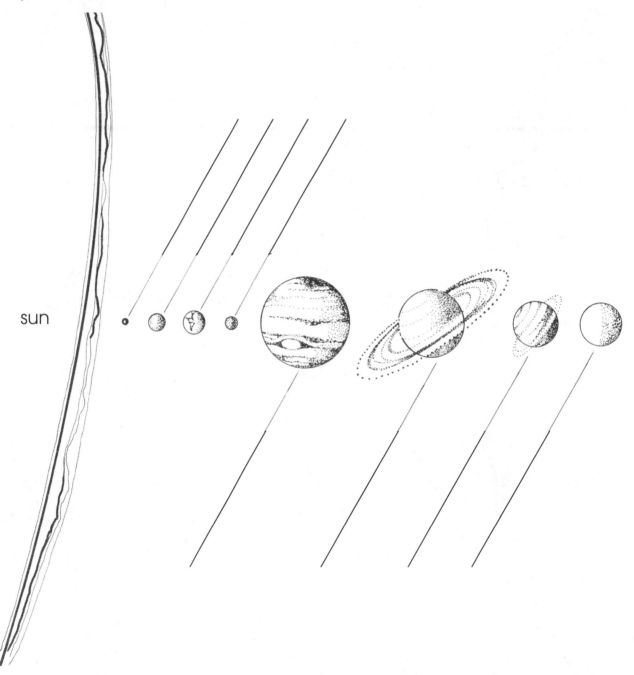

sun

| Earth | Mars | Neptune | Uranus |
| Jupiter | Mercury | Saturn | Venus |

The Inner Planets

The planets that are closest to the sun are called the **inner planets**.

Label the inner planets and the sun.

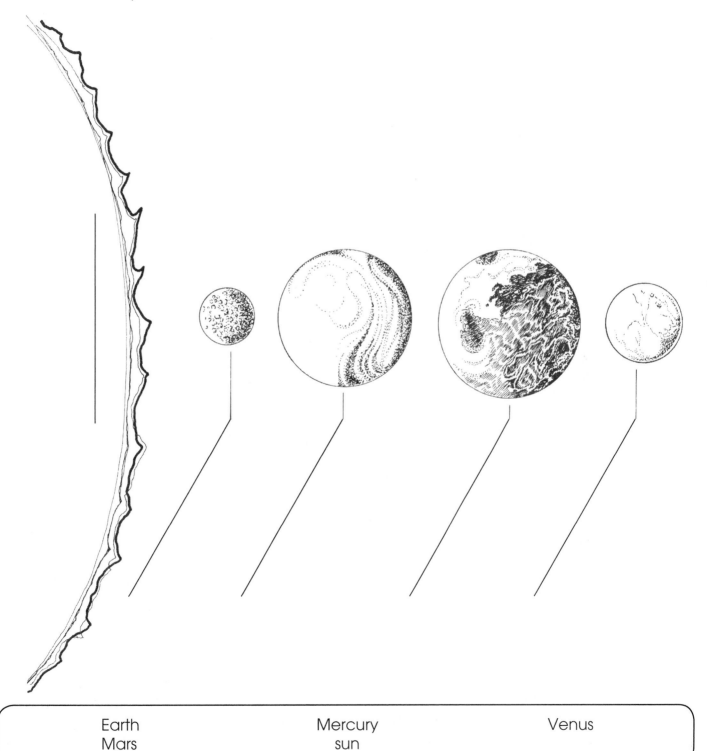

Earth	Mercury	Venus
Mars	sun	

The Outer Planets

The <u>planets that are farthest</u> from the sun are called the **outer planets**.

Label the outer planets.

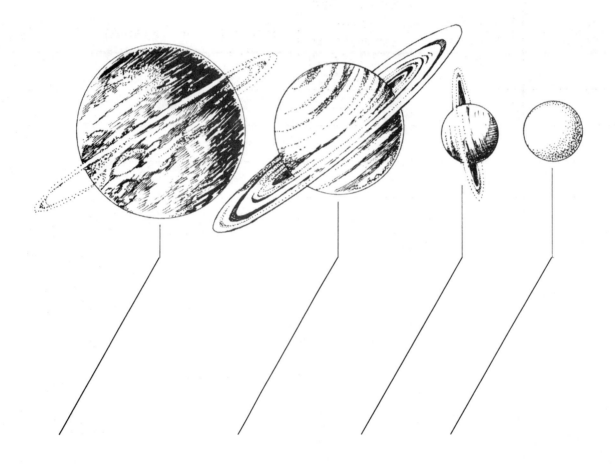

| Jupiter | Neptune | Saturn | Uranus |

Exporing Our Solar System

Comets, asteroids, and some meteors travel around the sun in our solar system. But, the largest objects traveling around the sun are the planets.

Use your science book, an encyclopedia, or an Internet source to complete the chart about the planets of our solar system.

Planet	Position from the Sun	Revolution Time (Length of Year—Earth Days)	Rotation Time	Known Satellites	Distance from the Sun (Miles)

Fill in the names of the planets.

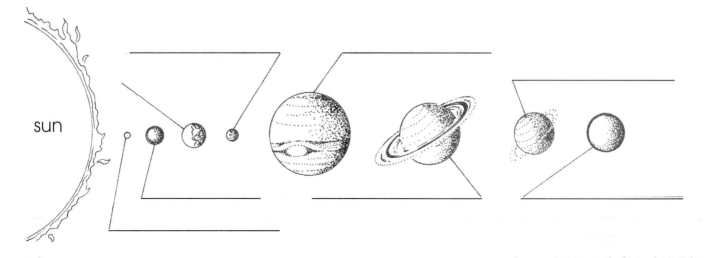

sun

Planets Crossword

Use what you have learned about the planets of our solar system to complete the puzzle. You may need to refer to your science book, an encyclopedia, or the Internet.

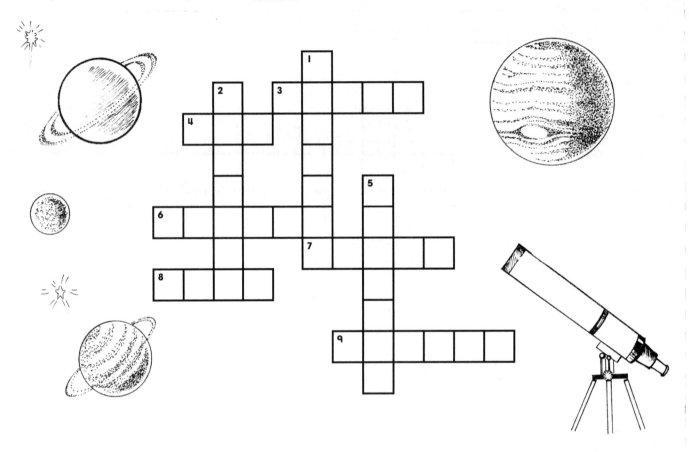

Across

3. I am the closest in size to Earth.
4. I am the star at the center of the solar system.
6. I have the greatest number of natural satellites.
7. I am the only planet known to support life.
8. I am known as the Red Planet.
9. I am the most distant planet that can be seen without a telescope.

Down

1. I am the eighth planet from the sun.
2. I am a large planet known for my "Great Red Spot."
5. I am the closet planet to the sun.

Earth	Mercury	sun
Jupiter	Neptune	Uranus
Mars	Saturn	Venus

Our Closest Star: The Sun

The sun is the closest star to Earth. It is a ball of glowing gases, and life on Earth would not be possible without it.

Label the different layers and features of the sun.

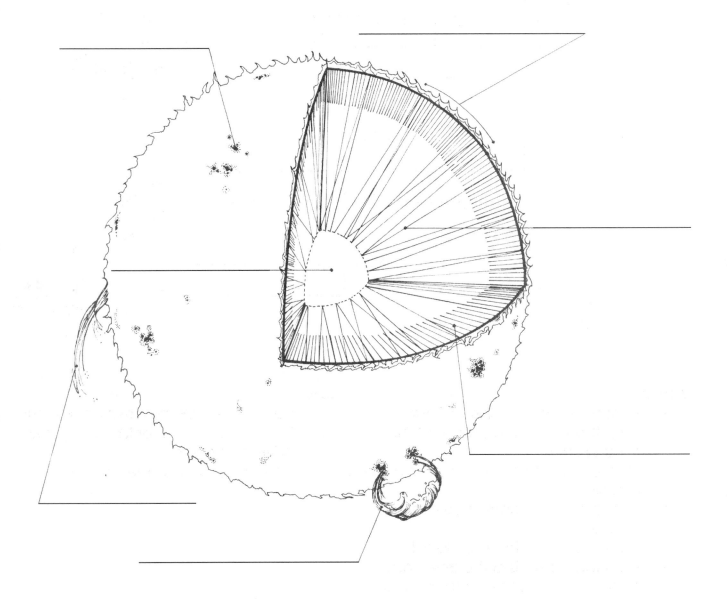

| chromosphere | flare | prominence | sunspot |
| core | photosphere | radiative zone | |

Name_____

Dirty Snowballs

Comets are like "dirty snowballs." They are frozen masses of gas and dust particles. On November 12, 2014, a probe named *Philae* landed on the first comet. After traveling in space for over 10 years, it will collect data and images to help scientists better understand comets.

Label the parts of the comet.

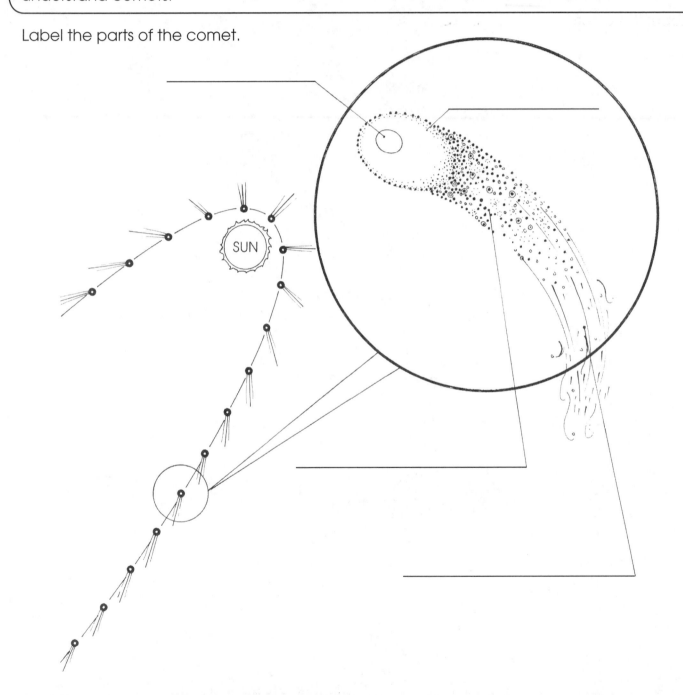

| coma | dust tail | gas tail | nucleus |

The Asteroid Belt

Scientists believe that asteroids may be pieces of a planet that was torn apart millions of years ago. Thousands of large asteroids have been tracked, but hundreds of thousands of smaller asteroids are in the asteroid belt.

Label the asteroid belt and the planets.

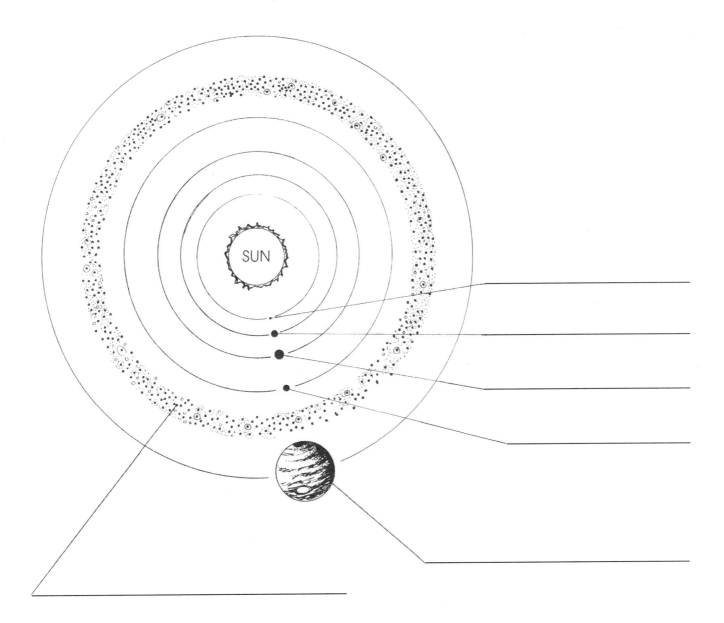

| asteroid belt | Jupiter | Mercury |
| Earth | Mars | Venus |

41

The North Star

As Earth rotates, all the stars in the sky appear to move from east to west. Because Polaris is directly above the North Pole, it does not move, and so it is also called the North Star.

Polaris is found in the constellation Ursa Minor, also called the Little Dipper. The Big Dipper is found in the constellation Ursa Major, also called the Great Bear.

Trace and label the Big Dipper and the Little Dipper. Label Polaris.

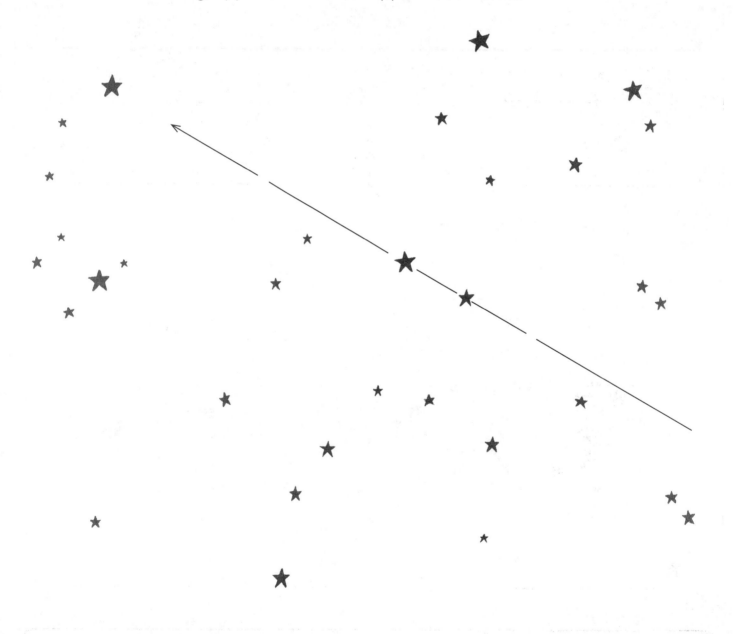

| Big Dipper | Little Dipper | Polaris |

Pictures in the Night Sky

For thousands of years, people from every culture have gazed into the night sky and imagined groups of stars outlining a picture. These star pictures, called **constellations**, are like giant dot-to-dot puzzles in the night sky.

Name each well-known constellation.

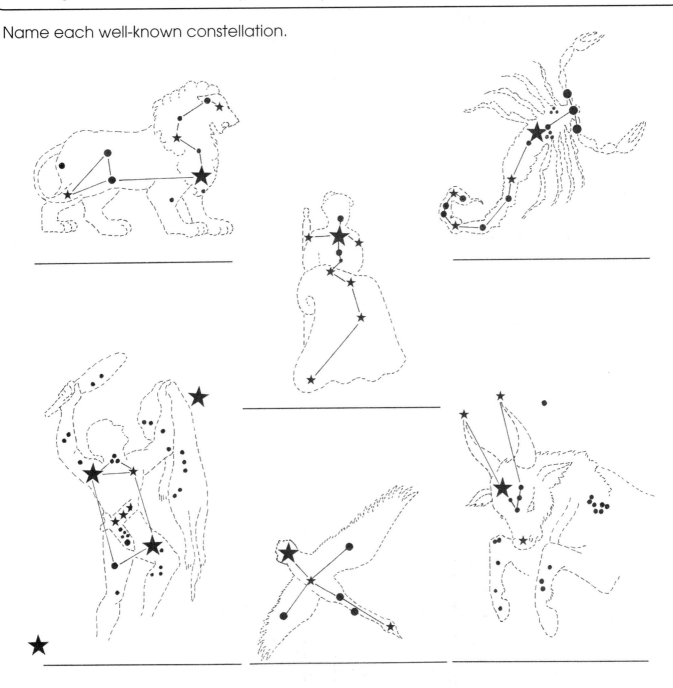

_____   _____

_____

_____   _____   _____

| Cassiopeia | Leo | Scorpio |
| Cygnus | Orion | Taurus |

Name_____

Galaxies

Beyond our galaxy lie billions of other galaxies. The Hubble telescope has enabled us to see into deep space.

Label the shapes of each galaxy.

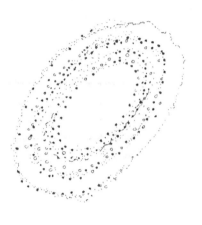

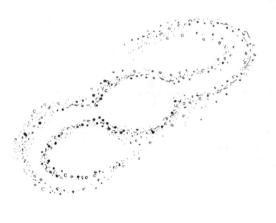

_____   _____

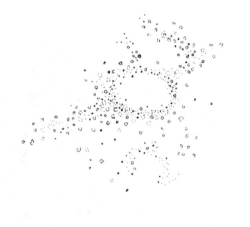

_____   _____

| barred spiral | elliptical | irregular | spiral |

Radio Telescope

Radio telescopes give us much information about the universe that other types of telescopes can't give. They can detect faint radio waves emitted by extraterrestrial sources.

Label the parts of the radio telescope.

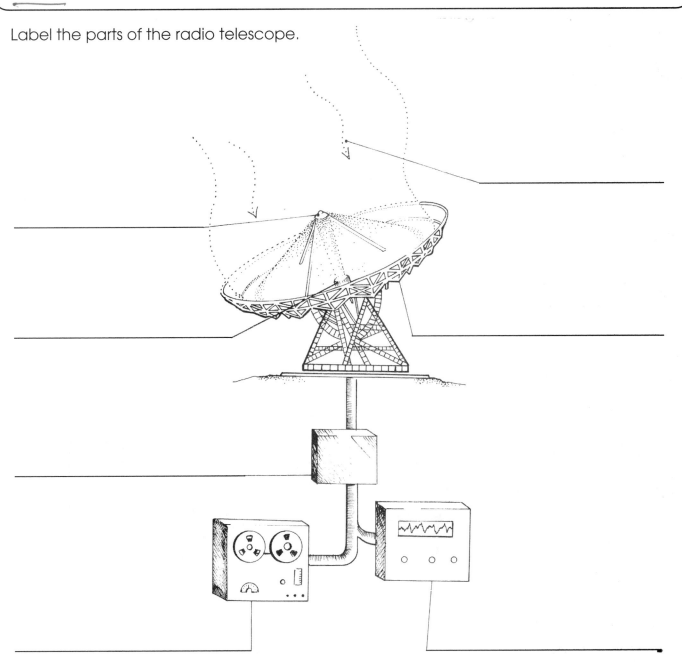

control unit	display unit	receiver	vertex box
computer	radio waves	reflector dish	

"Optic Glass"

In 1609, the Italian astronomer, Galilee, was the first person to see the heavenly bodies closer than they really were with his "optic glass," or telescope.

Label the refractor and reflector telescopes and their parts. You may use some words more than once.

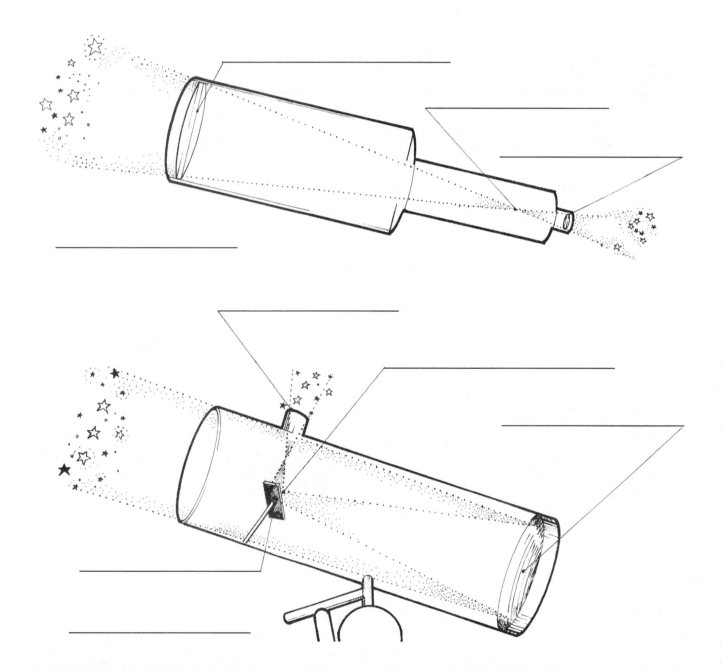

eyepiece lens	focal point	objective mirror	reflector telescope
flat mirror	objective lens	refractor telescope	

The Space Shuttle

Label the parts of the space shuttle.

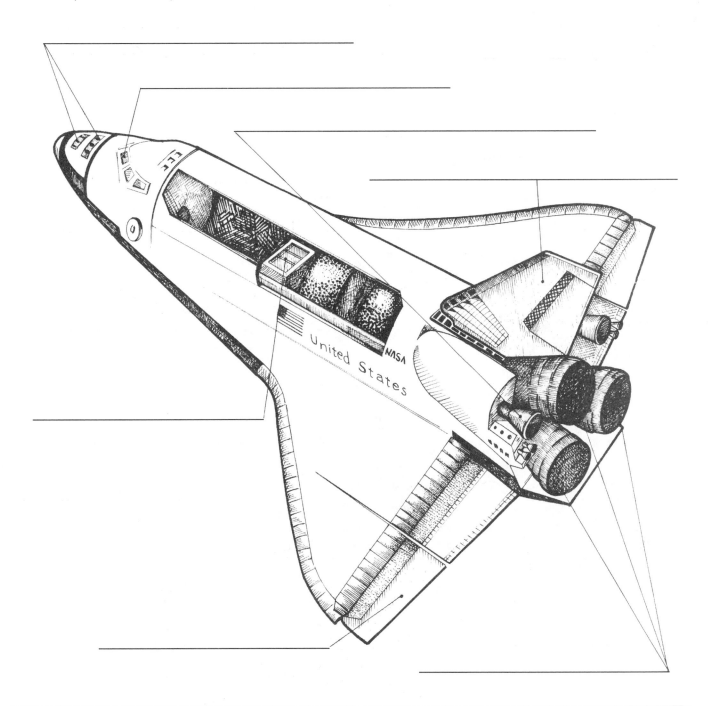

cockpit	payload bay
elevon	reaction control jets
main engines	rudder and speed brake
orbital maneuvering system engine	

Space Shuttle Launch Site

Label the parts of the space shuttle's launch site.

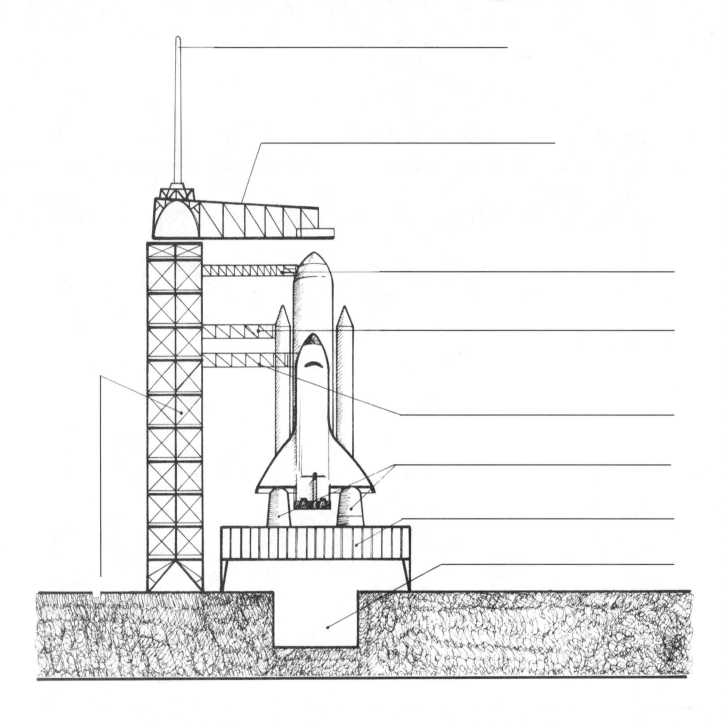

crane	launching pad platform	oxygen venting arm
flame platform	lightning mast	service structure
hydrogen venting arm	orbital access arm	tail service masts

The Flight of the Space Shuttle

Label the different phases of the space shuttle's mission.

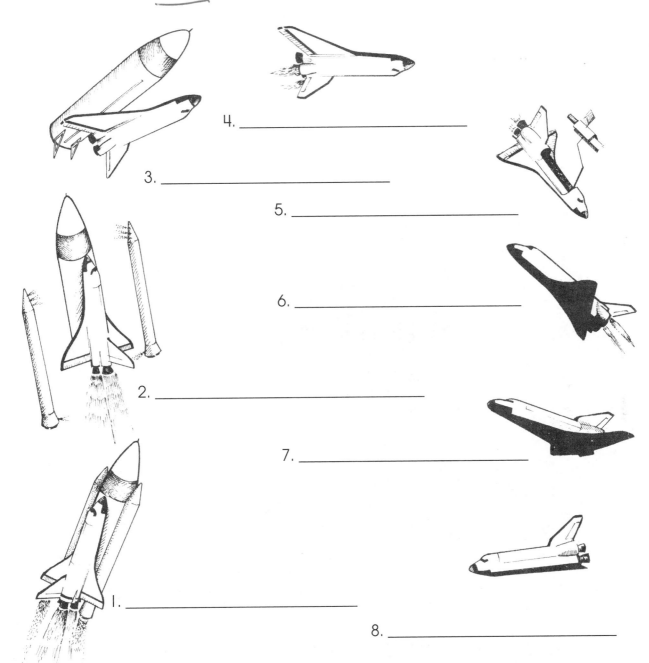

4. _____

3. _____

5. _____

6. _____

2. _____

7. _____

1. _____

8. _____

ascent	orbital activities
deorbit	orbit insertion
external tank separation	reentry
landing	solid rocket booster separation

Hemispheres

Earth is a giant sphere. When Earth is divided into two equal parts, each part is called a **hemisphere**.

Label the four hemispheres.

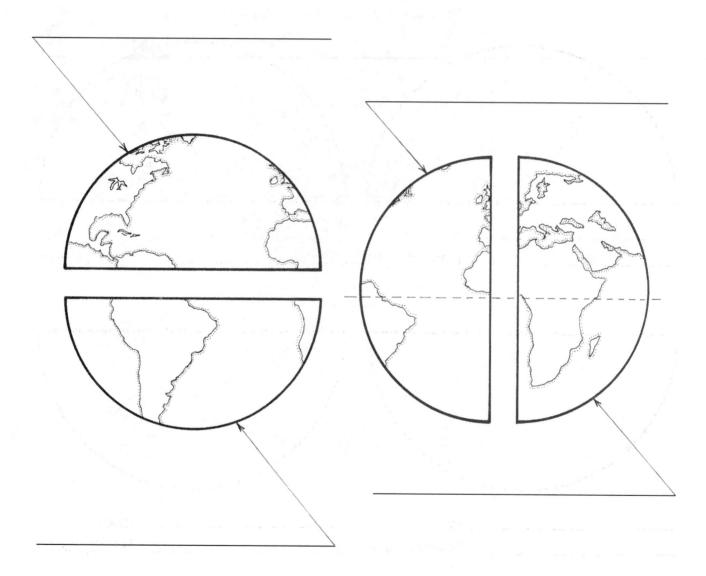

| Eastern Hemisphere | Southern Hemisphere |
| Northern Hemisphere | Western Hemisphere |

More Than One Hemisphere

You live in more than one hemisphere. Although it is impossible to live in the Northern and Southern Hemispheres or the Eastern and Western Hemispheres at the same time, it is possible to live in the Northern and Eastern, Northern and Western, Southern and Eastern, or Southern and Western Hemispheres.

Label the two hemispheres pictured in each image.

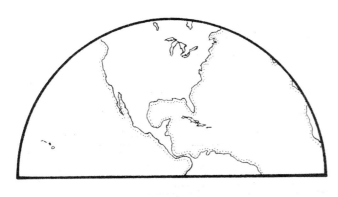

_____ and
_____ Hemispheres

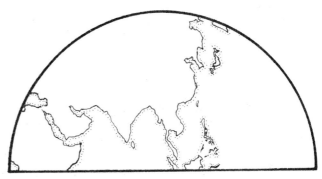

_____ and
_____ Hemispheres

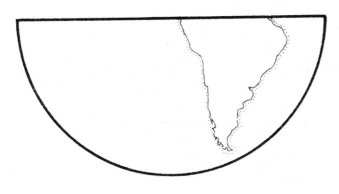

_____ and
_____ Hemispheres

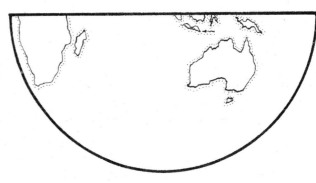

_____ and
_____ Hemispheres

| Eastern | Northern | Southern | Western |

Map Features

Everyone from the weather forecaster to a family on vacation finds maps as very valuable tools. But, they are useful only if you know how to use their many features.

Label the parts of the map. Then, explain the purpose of each.

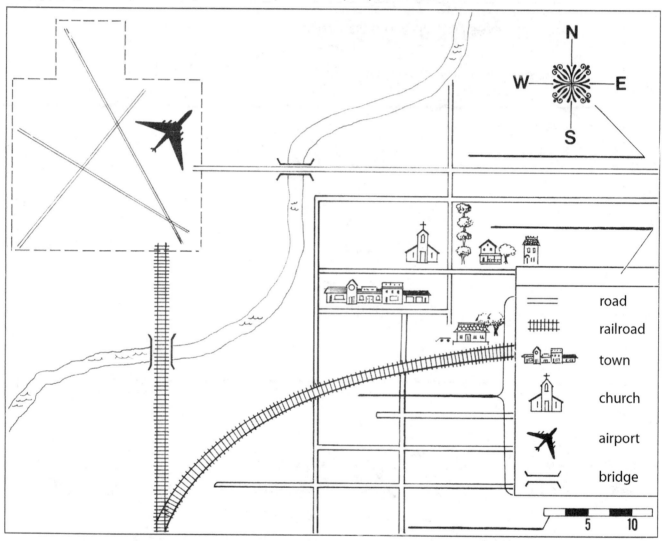

scale: _____

compass rose: _____

map legend: _____

symbols: _____

compass rose   map legend   scale   symbols

Using Latitude and Longitude

Use the latitude and longitude grid to pinpoint each location.

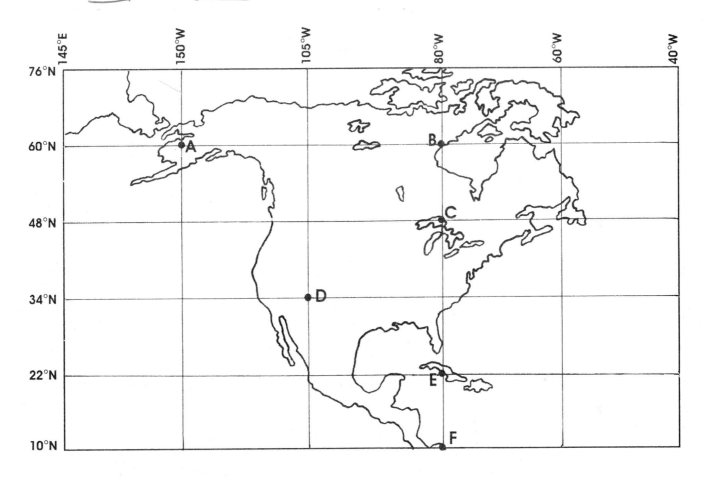

1. What is the latitude of ...

   point **A**? _____   point **D**? _____

   point **B**? _____   point **E**? _____

   point **C**? _____   point **F**? _____

2. What is the longitude of ...

   point **A**? _____   point **D**? _____

   point **B**? _____   point **E**? _____

   point **C**? _____   point **F**? _____

3. Give the location of ...

   point **A**. _____   point **D**. _____

   point **B**. _____   point **E**. _____

   point **C**. _____   point **F**. _____

Sea of Air

Our atmosphere extends several hundred kilometers upward. In the illustration, notice the different layers of the atmosphere and what may be found in each layer.

Label each of the layers and objects found in these layers.

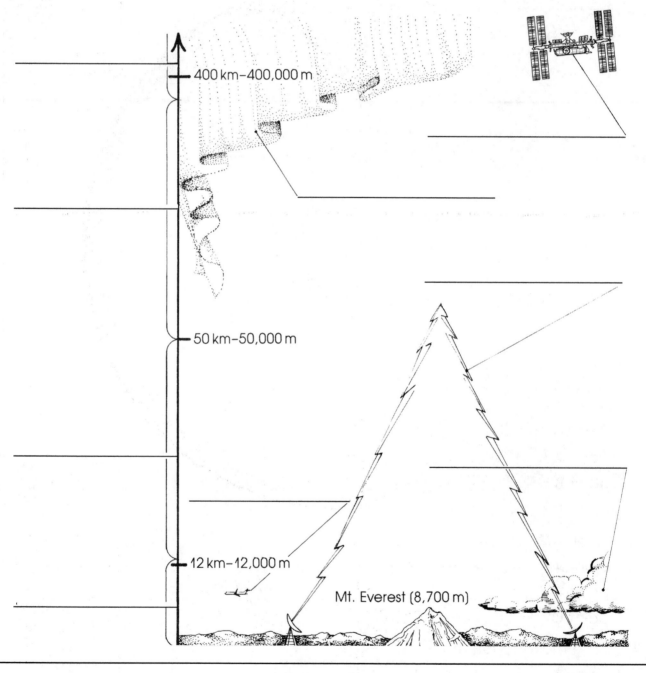

400 km–400,000 m

50 km–50,000 m

12 km–12,000 m

Mt. Everest (8,700 m)

aurorae	ionosphere	space station
exosphere	jet airplanes	stratosphere
highest clouds	radio waves	troposphere

The Center of Earth

Earth is composed of four different layers. Color the layers of Earth and the key.

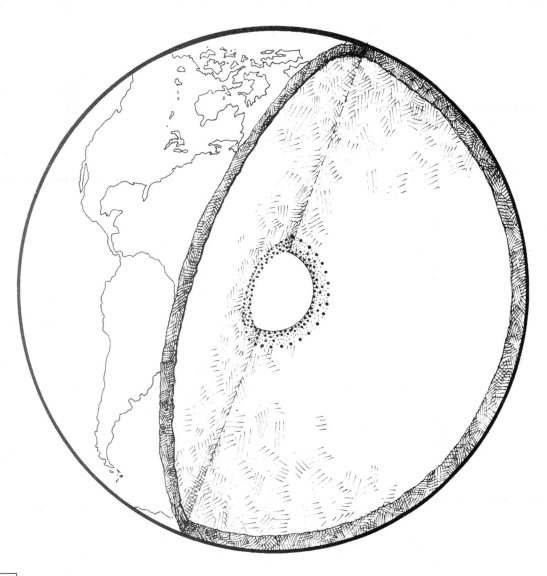

blue	water
green	land
brown	crust (5–70 km thick)
orange	mantle (3,000 km thick)
yellow	outer core (2,000 km thick)
red	inner core (1,500 km thick)

Solid to the Core

Label each layer of Earth.

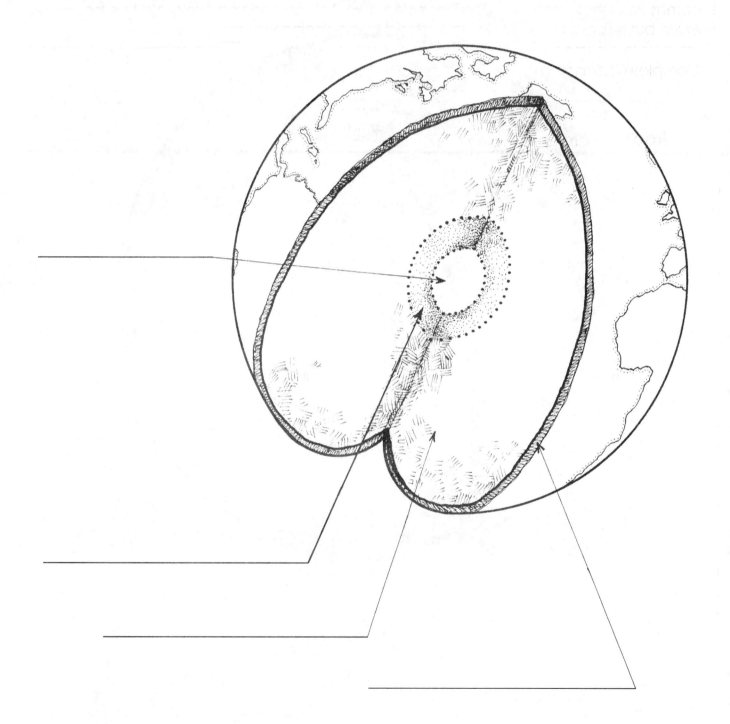

| crust | inner core | mantle | outer core |

The Rock Cycle

With the help of <u>heat</u>, pressure, and <u>weathering</u>, one type of rock can be changed into a new type of rock. For example, beautiful marble is formed from limestone, and slate comes from shale and clay. The changing of rocks is an ongoing cycle. No true beginning exists, but it might be easier to understand by beginning with magma.

Complete the rock cycle diagram.

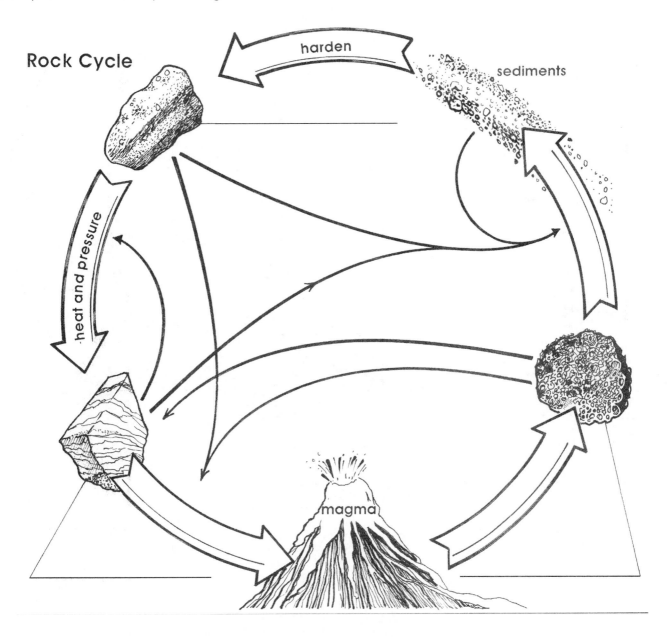

| cooling and hardening | melting | sedimentary rock |
| igneous rock | metamorphic rock | weathering |

Soil Profile

Examine the soild profile pictured. Identify the layer(s) where each of the following are found.

_____ live animals

_____ rock

_____ minerals

_____ live plants

_____ organic matter

_____ top layer

_____ middle layer

_____ lowest layer

_____ topsoil

_____ subsoil

_____ tree roots

_____ boulders

Making Crystals

Crystals come in a wide variety of shapes, colors, and sizes. People have always been fascinated by their incredible beauty.

Cut out each of the crystal patterns on the solid line. Then, fold along the dotted lines. Tape the sides together. Match the common crystal shapes drawn here with the ones you have created.

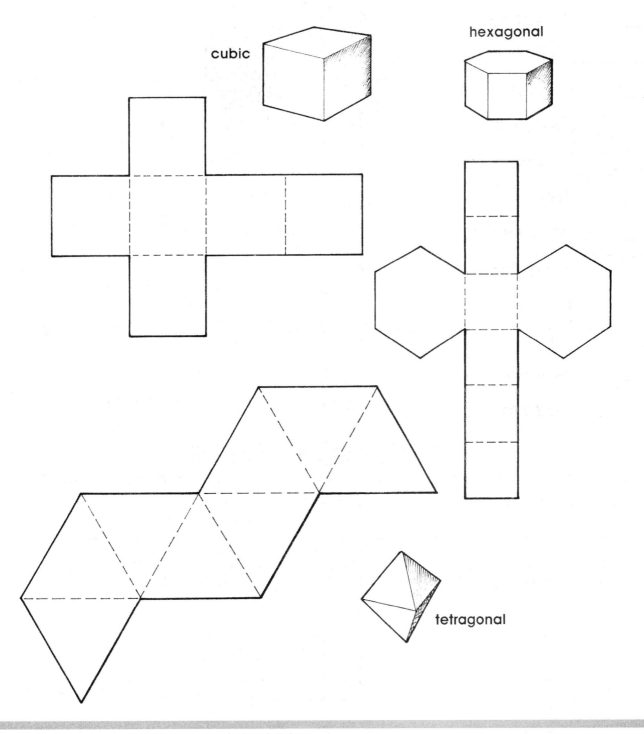

cubic

hexagonal

tetragonal

Mohs' Hardness Scale

One of the most useful properties applied in the identification of a mineral is its hardness. The **Mohs' hardness scale** measures a mineral's hardness by a simple scratch test.

Name the mineral that belongs in each step of the Mohs' hardness scale chart.

Mohs' Hardness Scale		
Hardness	**Mineral**	**Common Tests**
1		Fingernail will scratch it.
2		
3		Fingernail will not scratch it; a copper penny will.
4		Knife blade or window glass will scratch it.
5		
6		Will scratch a steel knife or window glass.
7		
8		
9		
10		Will scratch all common materials.

apatite   corundum   fluorite   talc
calcite   diamond   gypsum   topaz
feldspar/orthoclase   quartz

Name That Mineral

One can identify minerals by carefully observing their physical characteristics. Some of these characteristics are:

Hardness—This is determined with a scratch test.
Color—Color depends on the substances that make up the crystals. It varies greatly.
Luster—This refers to how light reflects off the mineral.

Find the unknown minerals and fill in the chart.

Hardness Scale		
Hardness	**Mineral**	**Common Tests**
1	talc	Fingernail will scratch it.
2	gypsum, kaolinite	
3	mica, calcite	A copper penny will scratch it.
4	fluorite	Knife blade or window glass will scratch it.
5	apatite, hornblende	
6	feldspar	Will scratch a steel knife or window glass.
7	quartz	
8	topaz	
9	corundum	
10	diamond	Will scratch all common materials.

Color	Mineral
White	quartz, feldspar, calcite, kaolinite, talc
Yellow	quartz, kaolinite
Black	hornblende, mica
Gray	feldspar, gypsum
Colorless	quartz, calcite, gypsum

Luster	Mineral
Glassy	quartz, feldspar, hornblende
Pearly	mica, gypsum, talc
Dull	kaolinite

Hardness	Color	Luster	Mineral
It will scratch a steel knife or window glass.	yellow	glassy	
It will scratch a steel knife or window glass.	gray	glassy	
A copper penny will scratch it.	black	pearly	
A fingernail will scratch it.	white	pearly	
A knife blade or window glass will scratch it.	black	glassy	

Classy Rocks

Three main groups of rock exist: **igneous** rock, **metamorphic** rock, and **sedimentary** rock. Each of the pictured rocks belongs to one of these groups.

Complete the definitions. Then, identify which group each rock belongs to.

 granite

 gneiss

 marble

_____

 limestone

 shale

 basalt

_____

 sandstone

 slate

obsidian

_____

 conglomerate

_____

Kind of Rock	Definition
igneous	
sedimentary	
metamorphic	

Word Bank	Definitions		
igneous	layers of loose material that solidified	cooled magma	rock that has been changed into a new rock
metamorphic			
sedimentary			

Rocks and Minerals Crossword

Use your knowledge of rocks and minerals to complete the puzzle.

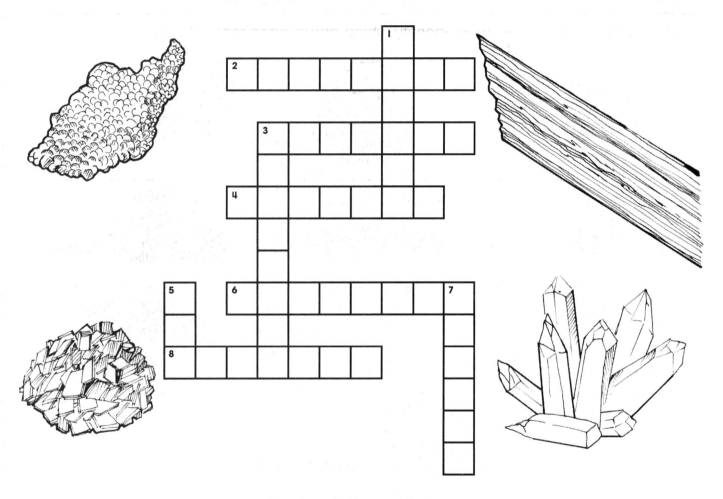

Across

2. An uneven break
3. Substance with 3-dimensional plane faces
4. Feel of a surface when rubbed
6. Measured with Mohs' scale
8. Quartz is an example of a _____.

Down

1. Light reflected from a mineral's surface
3. Smooth break in a mineral
5. Large mineral crystal with brilliant color
7. A _____ test shows the color of a mineral when it is rubbed into a fine powder.

cleavage	gem	mineral
crystal	hardness	streak
fracture	luster	texture

Name_____

Whose Fault Is It?

A crack in Earth's bedrock is called a **fault**. Two types of faults exist: the **strike-slip fault** and the **normal**, or **dip-slip fault**.

California is known for the San Andreas Fault. Draw the San Andreas Fault on the map of California. Then, label the two different kinds of faults.

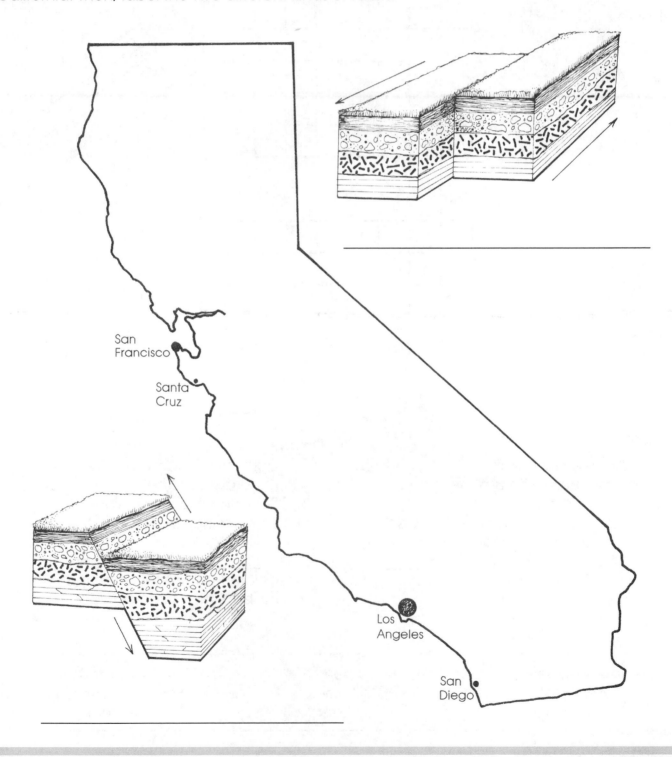

Name_____

Drifting Continents

About 250 million years ago, one continent existed, called Pangaea (Figure A).
By 45 million years ago, the land mass split into seven land masses (Figure B).

Label the land masses in Figure B.

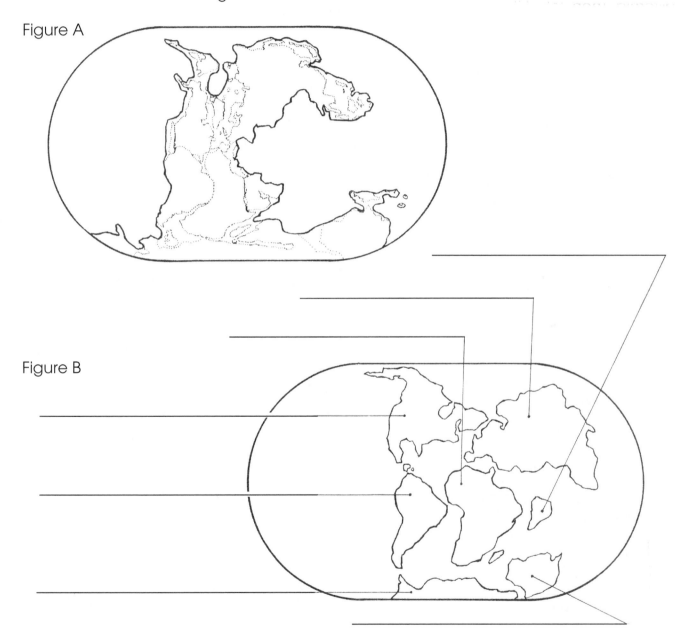

Figure A

Figure B

Africa	Australia	India	South America
Antarctica	Eurasia	North America	

Earth's Moving Plates

Earth's crust is made of rigid plates that are always moving. The boundaries of some plates are along the edges of the continents, while others are in the middle of the ocean. The map on this page shows the major plates near North and South America.

Using an encyclopedia, a textbook, or the Internet, label the eight plates.

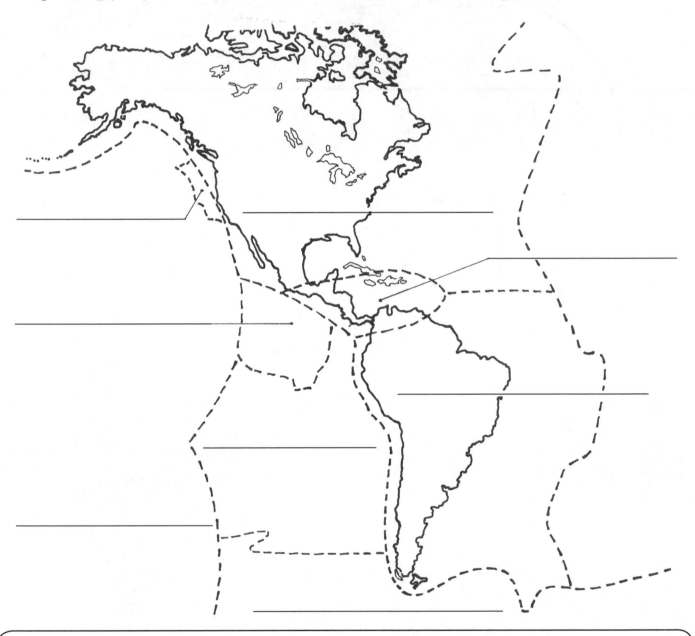

Antarctic Plate	Nazca Plate
Caribbean Plate	North American Plate
Cocos Plate	Pacific Plate
Juan de Fuca and Gorda Plates	South American Plate

"Broken Plates"

Below are puzzle pieces of Earth's seven major plates. Cut out the plates and glue them on a separate sheet of paper. Label the plates.

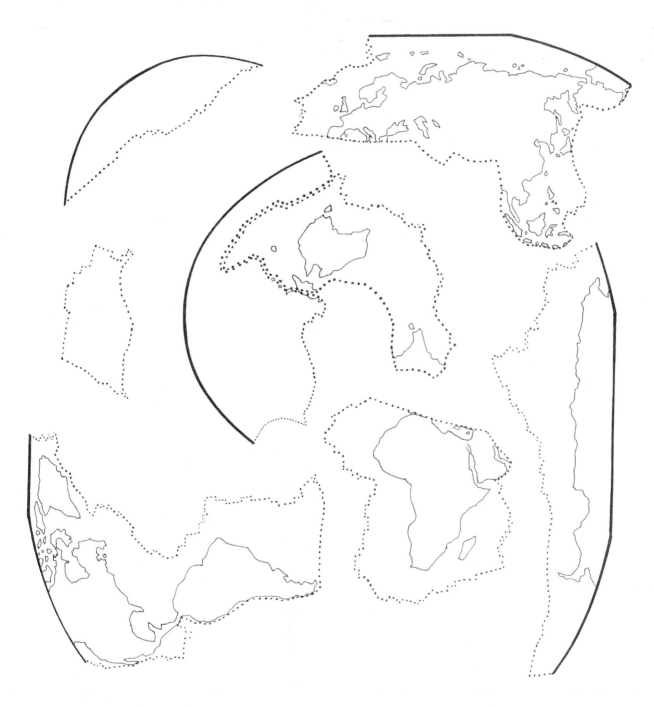

African Plate	Antarctic Plate	Nazca Plate
American Plate	Eurasian Plate	Pacific Plate
	Indo-Australian Plate	

Bending Earth's Crust

According to the theory of plate tectonics, Earth's crust is broken into about 20 **plates**. These plates are slowly moving. The edges of some plates are moving toward each other. A **trench** is formed when one plate bends and dives under another. The diving edge then descends into Earth's hot **mantle** and starts melting into magma. The **magma** can then rise and break through Earth's crust bursting out of a **volcano**. The edge of the overriding plate crumples, resulting in a mountain range.

Label the diagram.

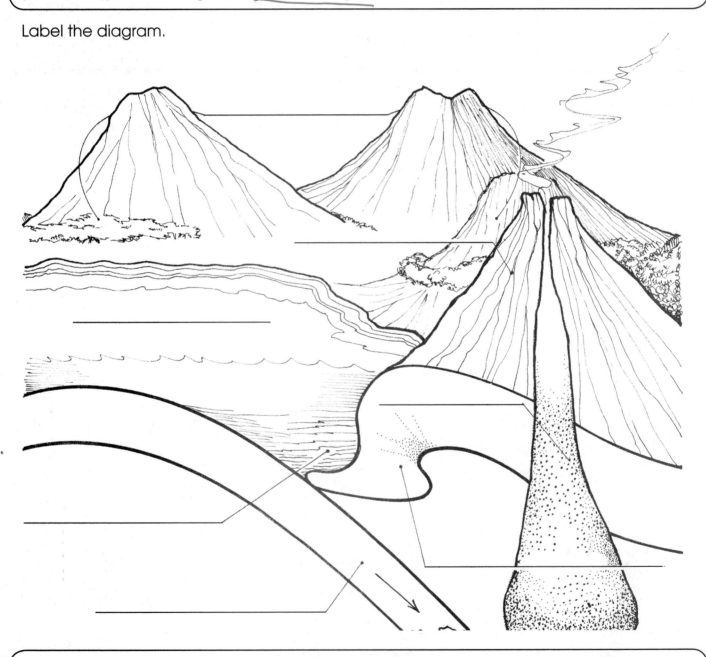

descending plate	mountains	overriding plate	volcano
magma	ocean	trench	

Volcanoes

Label the parts of the volcano.

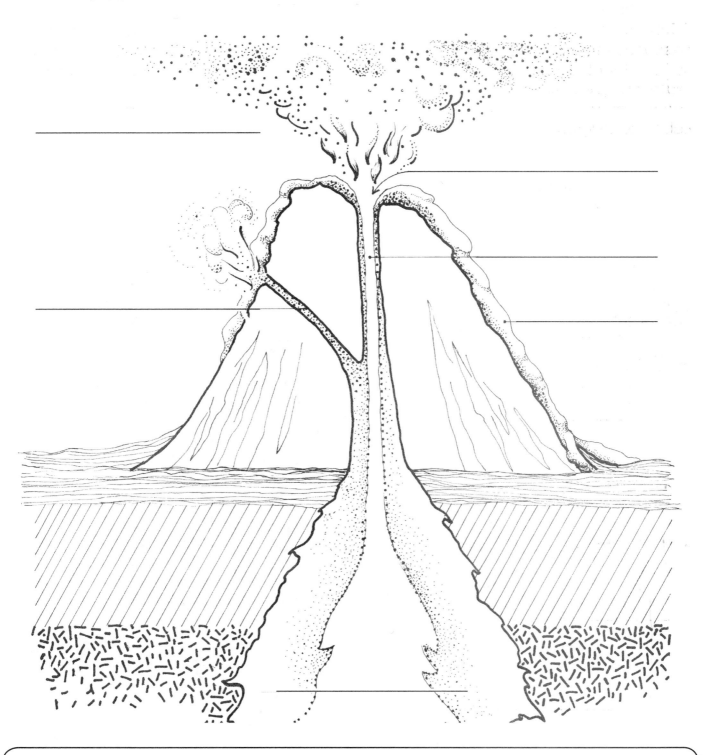

central vent	gas and dust	magma chamber
conduit	lava	side vent

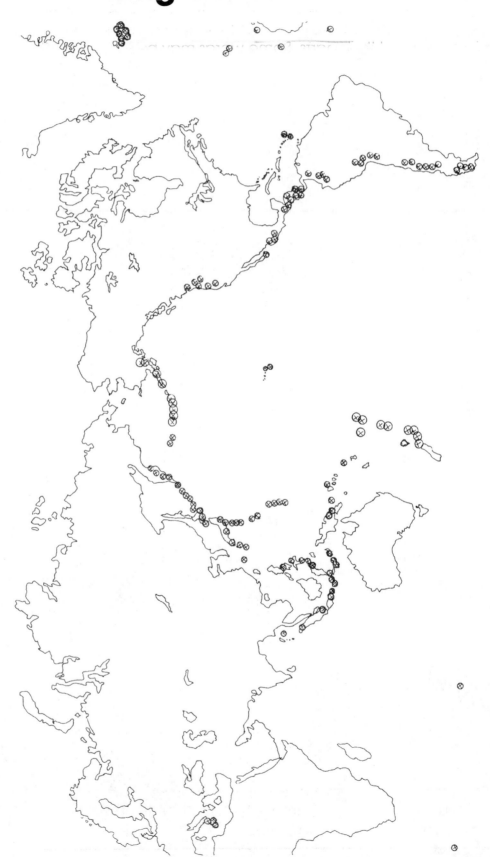

Ring of Fire

More than 500 active volcanoes exist in the world. More than half of these encircle the Pacific Ocean in an area called the **Ring of Fire**.

Color the region known as the Ring of Fire. Research this region. Locate and label some of its well-known volcanoes.

Volcanic Cones

Volcanic cones can be classified by their shapes. Label the three different kinds of volcanic cones and their parts. Some words may be used more than once.

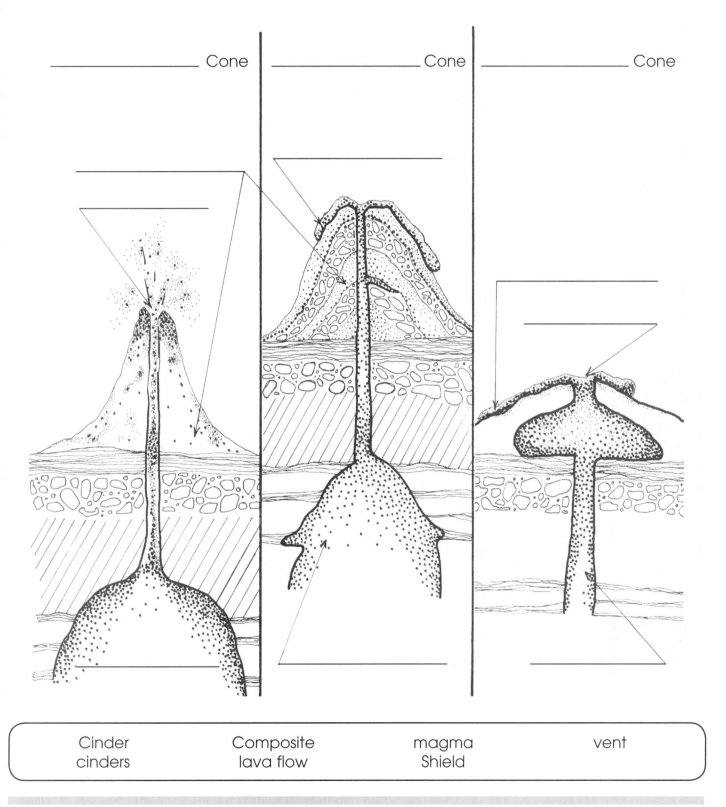

_____ Cone   _____ Cone   _____ Cone

Cinder	Composite	magma	vent
cinders	lava flow	Shield	

Forming Igneous Rock

Igneous rock is one of the three major types of rock, formed by the hardening of molten rock (magma). Magma does not always reach Earth's surface as erupting lava. It can form other igneous rock structures underground.

Label the igneous rock structures.

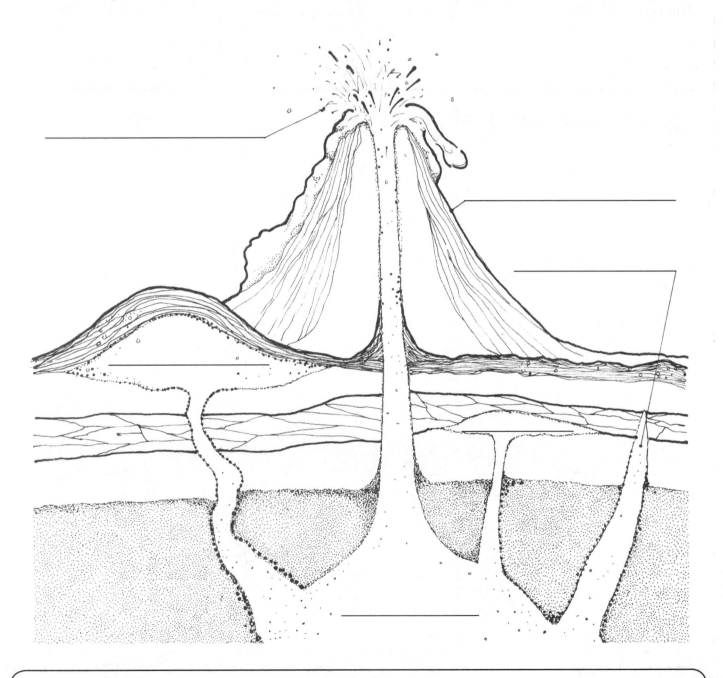

batholith	laccolith	sill
dike	lava	volcano

Drilling for Oil

Most oil is found thousands of feet beneath the surface of the earth. Trapped beneath layers of nonporous rock, such as shale, oil cannot reach the surface. Pockets of natural gas will often form where oil is. Oil companies drill for oil using large drills that grind through layers of soil and bedrock.

The illustration shows one example of how oil can be found. Label the illustration.

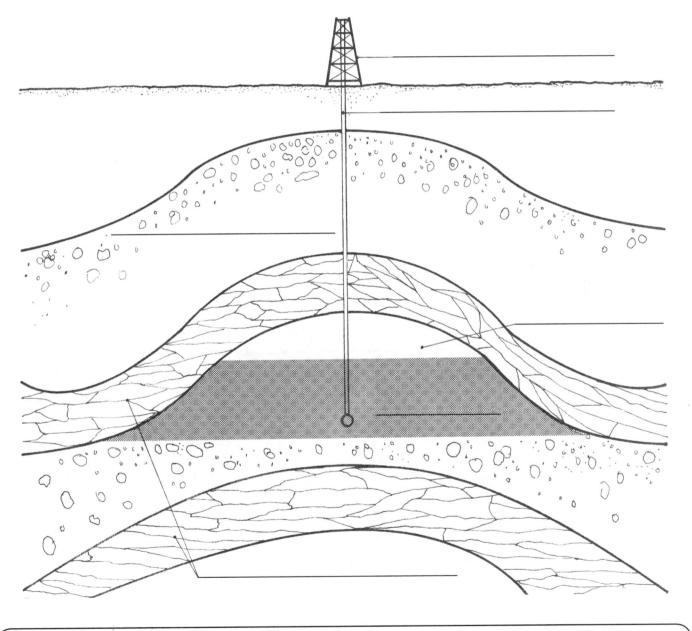

derrick	natural gas	oil
drill pipe	nonporous rock	porous rock

Coral Reefs

Three types of coral reefs are pictured. Label each type of coral reef and the feature that is enclosed by the reef. Then, number the steps in the formation of an atoll.

_____

Step No. _____

_____

_____

Step No. _____

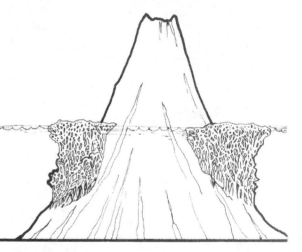

_____

_____

Step No. _____

atoll	fringing reef	island
barrier reef	inactive volcano	lagoon

Groundwater at Work

Groundwater is water located beneath the surface in pore spaces, fractures, and open formations. People remove groundwater with wells.

Label each diagram.

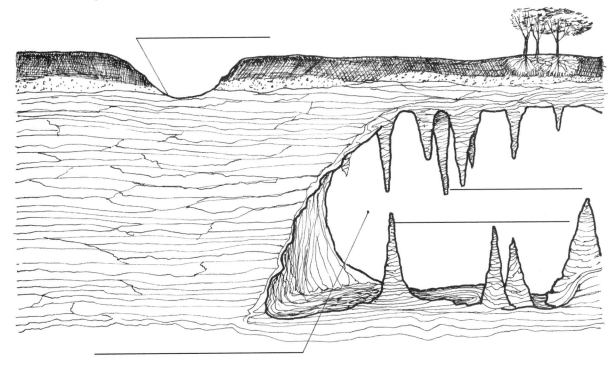

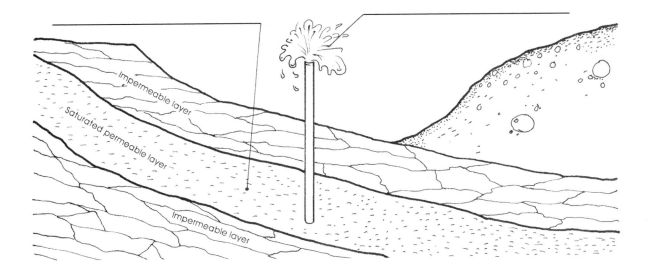

aquifer	cave	stalactite
artesian well	sinkhole	stalagmite

The Ocean Floor

Label the features of the ocean floor.

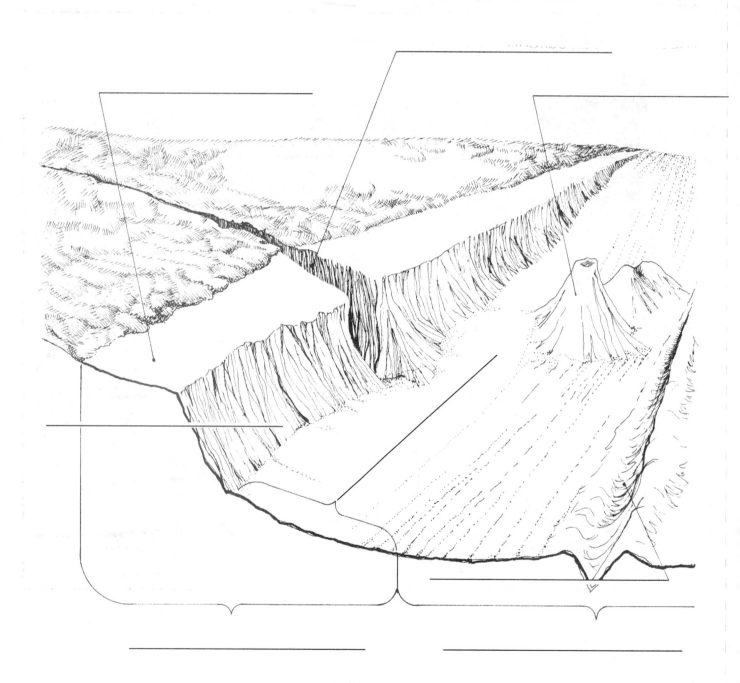

Ocean Currents

Water moves within the oceans in streams called **currents**. Several major currents are always present in the world's oceans.

Label the ocean currents pictured on the map.

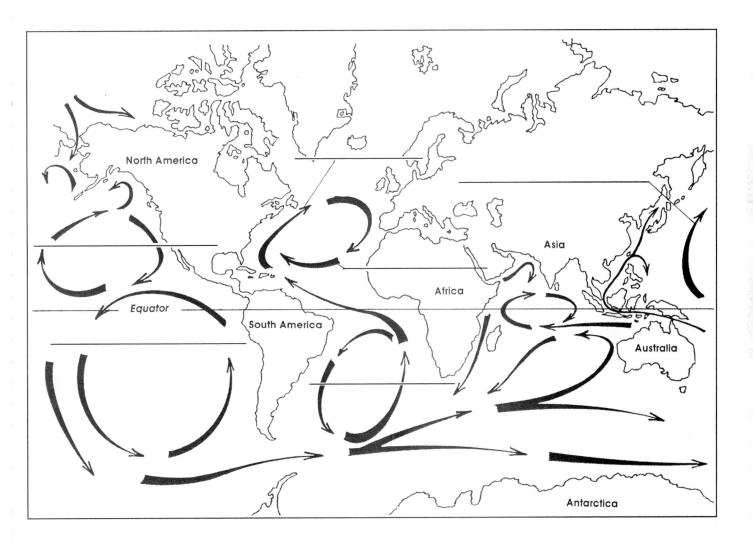

| Brazil Current | Canary Current | Kuroshio (Japan) Current |
| California Current | Gulf Stream | Peru Current |

Landform Regions of the United States

The continental United States can be divided into several major landform regions.
Label each region.

Appalachian Highlands
Coastal Lowlands
Colorado Plateau
Columbia Plateau

Great Basin
Interior Plains
Pacific Ranges and Lowlands
Rocky Mountains

Topographic Maps

A **topographic map** uses contour lines to show the elevation and slope of hills, valleys, and other natural features.

Label the various land features and elements of the topographic map.

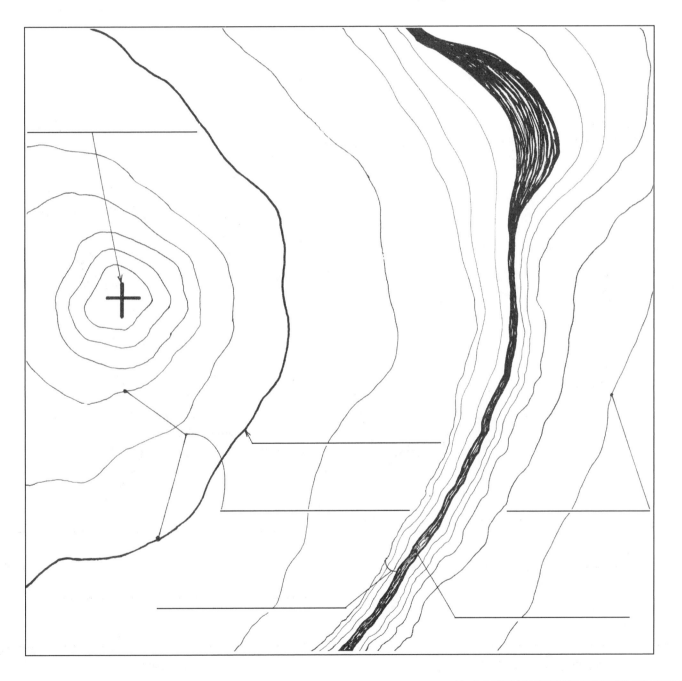

contour line	index contour line	river
gentle slope	mountain top	steep slope

Benchmark to Benchmark

Use the benchmarks on the map to help you draw the contour lines. The contour lines should be drawn at 20-foot intervals.

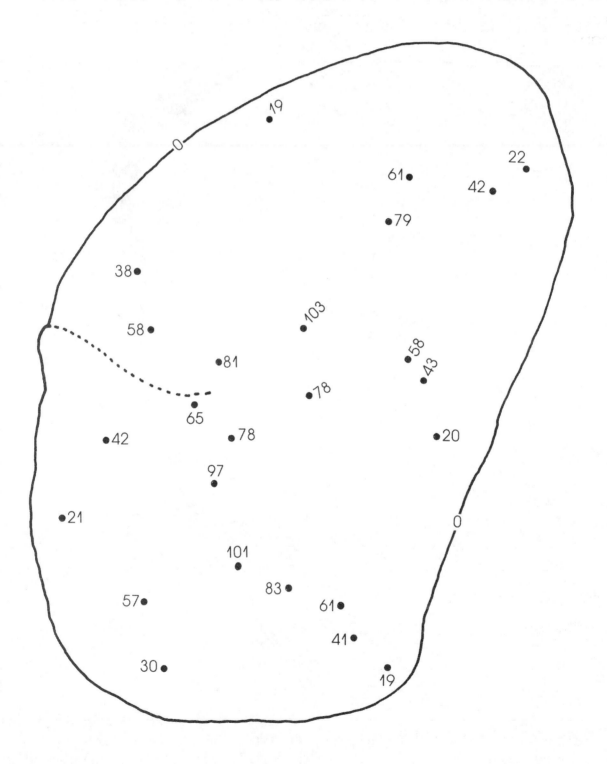

Reading Topographic Maps

Topographical maps give the geographical positions and elevations of both manmade and natural features.

Using the contour lines and contour intervals, label the elevations of the features on this map.

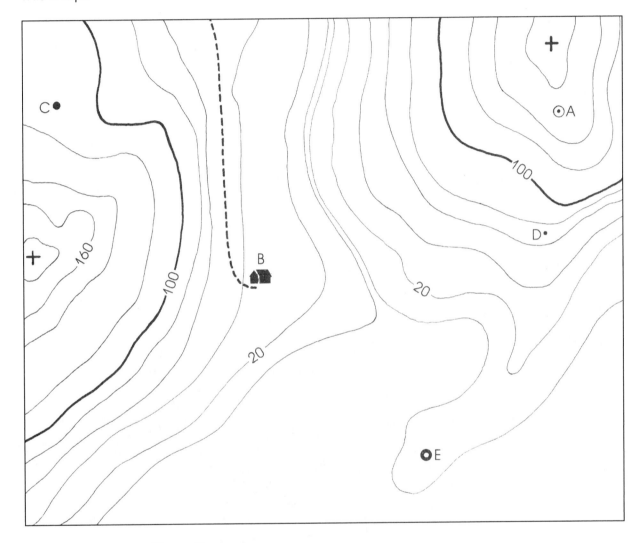

Feature   Elevation

A.   between _____ and _____ feet

B.   between _____ and _____ feet

C.   between _____ and _____ feet

D.   between _____ and _____ feet

E.   between _____ and _____ feet

Meandering River

A river goes through different stages of development as it erodes its channel.

Label the parts of the river.

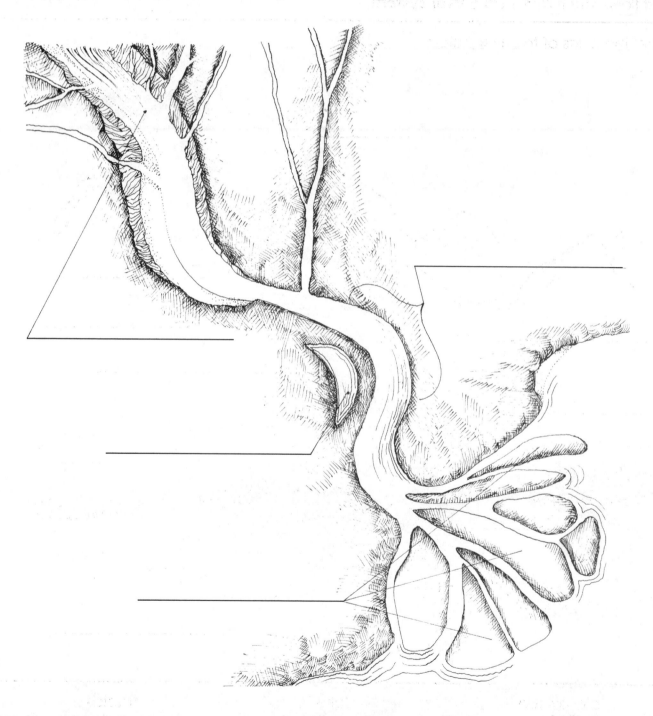

delta   meander   oxbow lake   young river

River System

A river may begin its journey to the sea high up in the mountains as a melting glacier, or as a number of small streams and brooks. As the river flows downhill, the moving water reshapes the land by carrying away sand, stones, and clay. The river and all the water that flows into it make up a **river system**.

Label the parts of the river system.

alluvial fan	lake	rapids
delta	meander	tributary
glacier	oxbow lake	waterfall

Glaciers

Tons of ice and trapped rock scrape and grind mountain walls as a glacier creeps down a mountain. The tremendous force of the moving glacier reshapes the mountain slopes in its path, leaving behind deposits of rock.

Label the formations made by the moving glacier.

| cirque | drumlins | kettle lake |
| crevasses | esker | terminal moraine |

You're All Wet

It's a wet day! The symbols on the weather map show eight different forms of precipitation occuring around the country. Label each form of precipitation.

| drizzle | hail | shower | snow |
| fog | rain | sleet | thunderstorm |

Gentle Breezes

On the chart, fill in the wind speed and wind direction for each city.

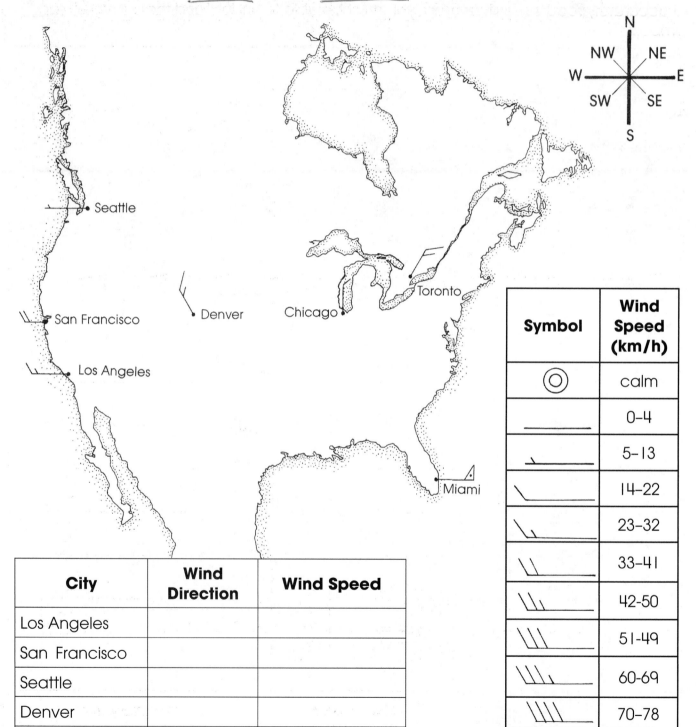

City	Wind Direction	Wind Speed
Los Angeles		
San Francisco		
Seattle		
Denver		
Chicago		
Toronto		
Miami		

Symbol	Wind Speed (km/h)
◎	calm
	0–4
	5–13
	14–22
	23–32
	33–41
	42–50
	51–49
	60–69
	70–78
	79–87
	88–96

Weather Map Symbols

Weather maps provide data from which meteorologists prepare <u>weather forecasts</u>.
To accurately read a weather map, you must be able to understand the weather map symbols.

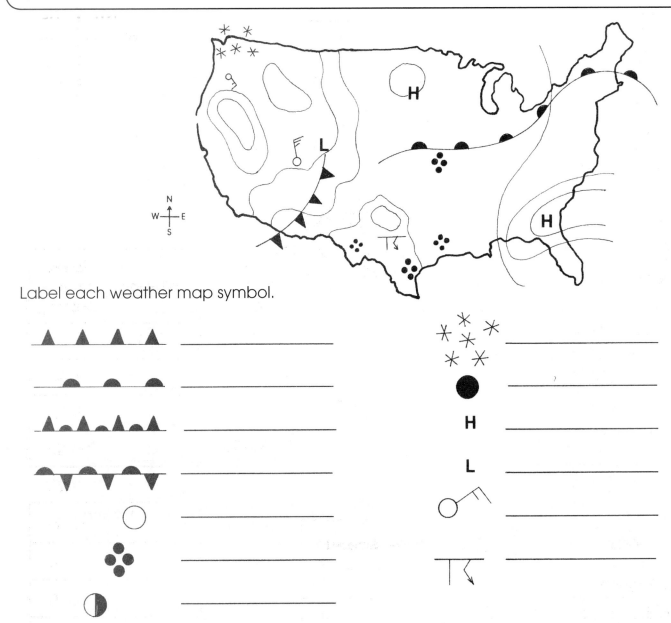

Label each weather map symbol.

_____

_____

_____

_____

_____

_____

H _____

L _____

_____

_____

_____

clear skies	low pressure	stationary front
cloudy	occluded front	thunderstorm
cold front	partly cloudy	warm front
high pressure	rain	wind speed and direction
	snow	

Using a Weather Map

Weather maps show the recorded weather conditions over a large geographic area.

Use the map along with what you have learned about weather symbols to complete the chart.

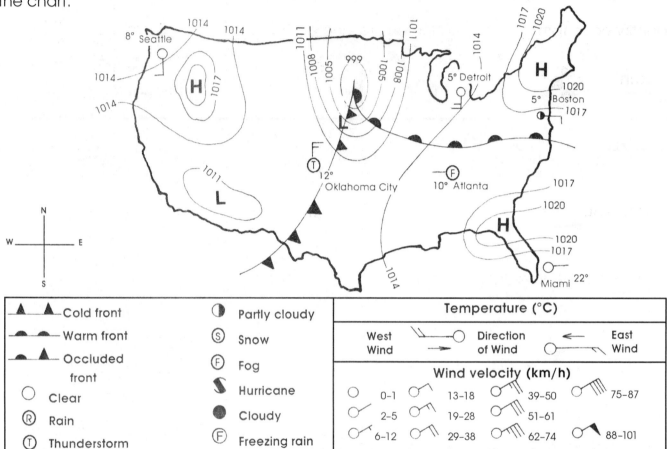

City	Temp.	Cloud Cover/ Weather Condition	Wind Velocity (km/h)	Wind Direction
Seattle				
Atlanta				
Detroit				
Miami				
Oklahoma City				
Boston				

Name_____

Precipitation

Precipitation is water vapor that condenses and falls to Earth. Depending on conditions in the atmosphere, precipitation can fall in a number of forms. The symbol for each form is pictured.

Identify each form of precipitation by drawing its symbol next to its description.

rain

drizzle

rain showers

sleet

snow

hail

fog

Symbol	Definition
	Clouds that form close to the ground.
	Droplets that freeze as they get closer to the ground.
	Light mist of droplets falling to Earth.
	Droplets of water freeze around ice crystals as they bounce up and down within a storm cloud and fall to Earth when they get heavy.
	Vapor that changes directly into crystalline flakes because of freezing temperatures.
	Water vapor that forms droplets and falls to Earth.
	Large amount of droplets falling to Earth.

Use another source to help you complete the chart.

Weather	Symbol	Definition
thunderstorm		
lightning		
squall		

Moving Weather Systems

A careful study of daily weather maps will show that weather systems are constantly on the move. You will need four copies of this page. Use a new sheet every day for three days to copy that day's weather pattern (frontal systems, pressure cells, and precipitation) from your newspaper or the Internet. Study the movement of the pattern. Then, draw a weather pattern predicting where the weather systems will move on the next day.

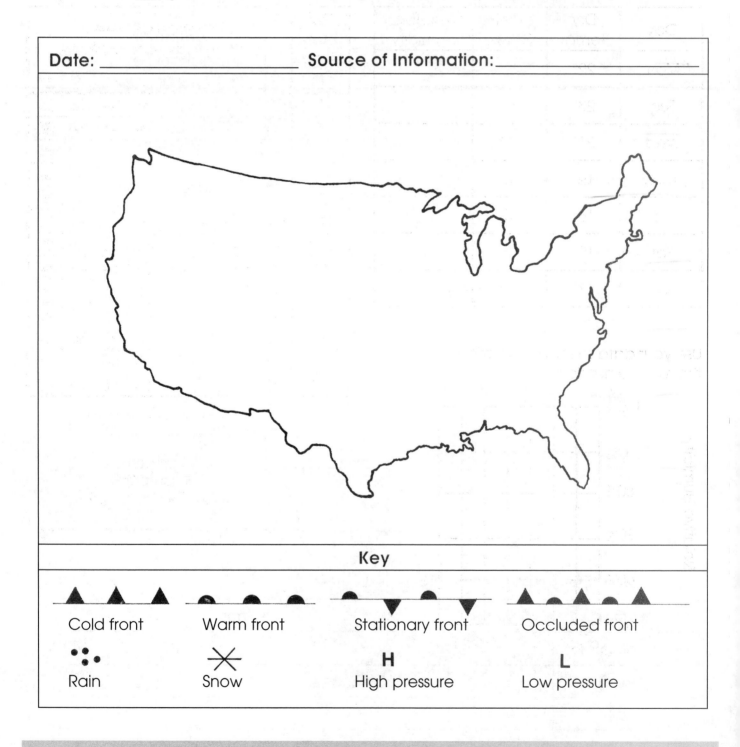

Date: _____ **Source of Information:**_____

Key

Cold front   Warm front   Stationary front   Occluded front

Rain   Snow   **H** High pressure   **L** Low pressure

Name_____

Relative Humidity

Relative humidity is the amount of water vapor that the air can hold at a certain temperature. Relative humidity is measured with a hygrometer and is a percentage.

Use the table to find the relative humidity for the data recorded on the chart.

Day	Dry Temp.	Wet Temp.	Relative Humidity
Mon.	22°	22°	
Tue.	23°	21°	
Wed.	21°	19°	
Thur.	19°	18°	
Fri.	18°	15°	
Sat.	19°	15°	
Sun.	17°	13°	

Dry bulb temp. (°C)	Difference between wet and dry temperatures							
	1°	2°	3°	4°	5°	6°	7°	8°
15°	90	80	71	61	53	44	36	27
16°	90	81	71	63	54	46	38	30
17°	90	81	72	64	55	47	40	32
18°	91	82	73	65	57	49	41	34
19°	91	82	74	65	58	50	43	36
20°	91	83	74	66	59	51	44	37
21°	91	83	75	67	60	53	46	39
22°	92	83	76	68	61	54	47	40
23°	92	84	76	69	62	55	48	42
24°	92	84	77	69	62	56	49	43
25°	92	84	77	70	63	57	50	44
26°	92	85	78	71	64	58	51	46
27°	92	85	78	71	65	58	52	47

Use your data to make a graph of the relative humidity.

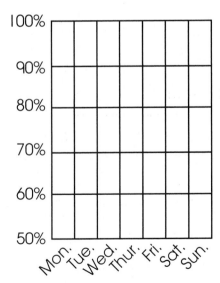

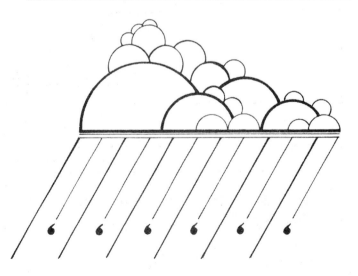

Air Currents

Name the three air current phenomena pictured. Then, fill in each explanation.

This picture shows _____.

Explanation: _____

_____

_____

_____

_____

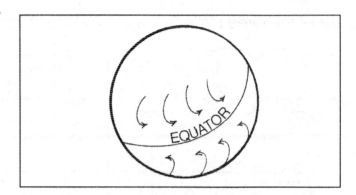

This picture shows _____.

Explanation: _____

_____

_____

_____

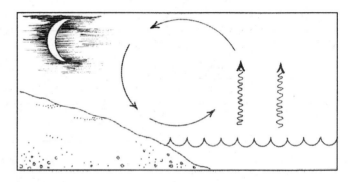

This picture shows _____.

Explanation: _____

_____

_____

_____

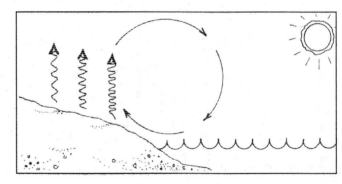

Phenomena	**Explanations**		
a land breeze	Earth's rotation affects the paths of winds.	During the day, cooler air from the sea replaces warm air over the shore.	At night, cool air over the shore replaces warm air over the sea.
a sea breeze			
the Coriolis Effect			

The Water Cycle

The <u>continuous circulation of water on Earth from the oceans, to the air, and to the land</u> is called the **water cycle**.

Label the three major steps in the water cycle and explain how the water cycle works.

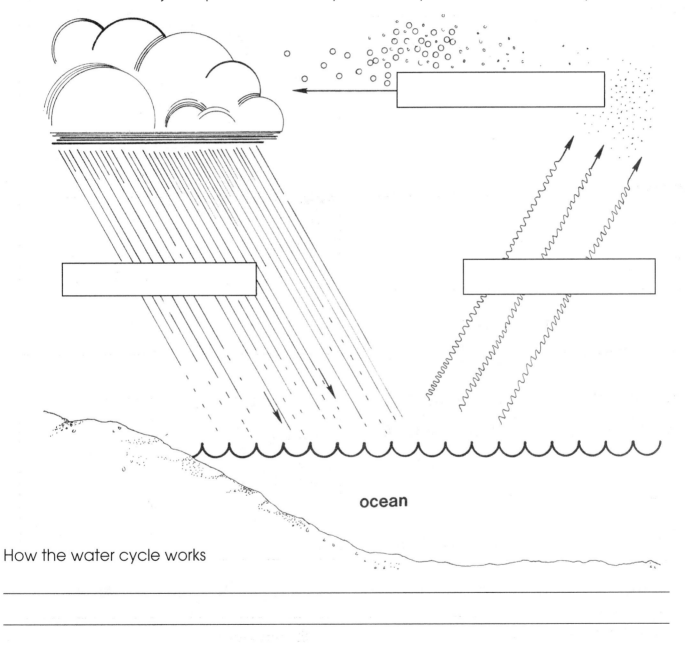

ocean

How the water cycle works

_____

_____

_____

_____

| condensation | evaporation | precipitation |

What's Up Front?

A **front** is where two air masses meet or converge. Changes in the weather take place along a front.

Label the two fronts and the kinds of air masses shown.

_____ front

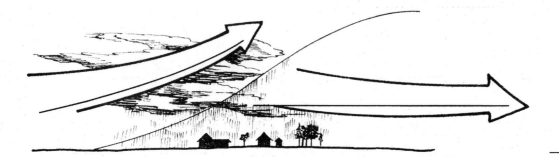

_____ front

Label the kind of front represented by each symbol.

_____ front _____ front _____ front _____ front

cold air mass	occluded	warm air mass
cold	stationary	warm

A Cold Front

This illustration shows a front between two air masses. The cooler air mass is replacing the warmer air mass.

Label the cloud types associated with the cold front.

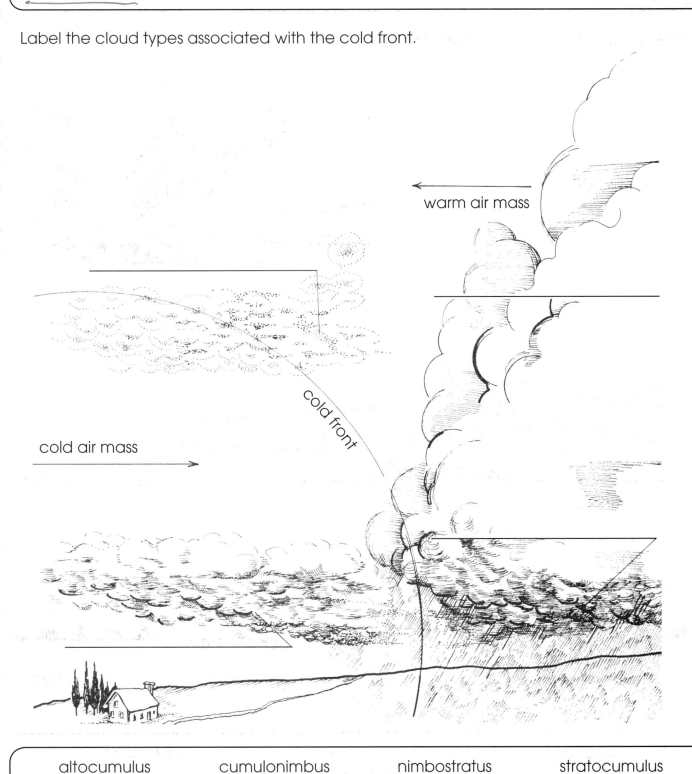

altocumulus   cumulonimbus   nimbostratus   stratocumulus

A Warm Front

This illustration is a front between two air masses. A warm air mass is pushing a cold air mass.

Label the cloud types associated with the warm front.

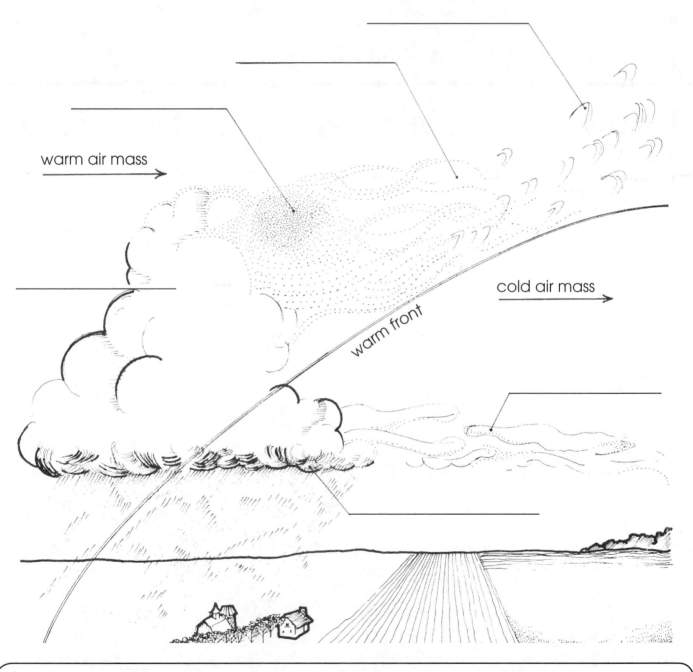

altostratus   cirrus   nimbostratus
cirrostratus   cumulus   stratus

Cloud Types

Label each cloud type shown.

altocumulus	cirrocumulus	cumulonimbus	stratocumulus
altostratus	cirrostratus	cumulus	stratus
	cirrus	nimbostratus	

Clouds and Weather

Different types of clouds are often associated with a specific kind of weather. Four different kinds of clouds are pictured. Write the name of the cloud type, a description of the cloud, and the kind of weather associated with each one.

Cloud Type	Name	Description	Associated Weather

cirrus	fair, sometimes showers	stratus
cumulonimbus	piles of "puffy" clouds	tall, dark, and billowing
cumulus	smooth sheets, or layers	thin, wispy clouds
fair	steady drizzle	thunderstorms

Name_____

Tomorrow's Weather Forecast

Check the accuracy of the weather forecasts in your area for the next week. Complete the chart by writing the forecast for tomorrow's weather and then recording the actual weather for that day. Indicate whether the forecast was accurate by circling *yes* or *no*.

	Date	Temp. Range	Precipitation	Wind Speed	Wind Direction	Sky Condition	Accurate Forecast?
Forecast							Yes
Actual							No
Forecast							Yes
Actual							No
Forecast							Yes
Actual							No
Forecast							Yes
Actual							No
Forecast							Yes
Actual							No
Forecast							Yes
Actual							No
Forecast							Yes
Actual							No

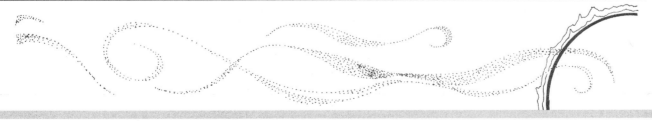

Weather Tools

Label each weather instrument.

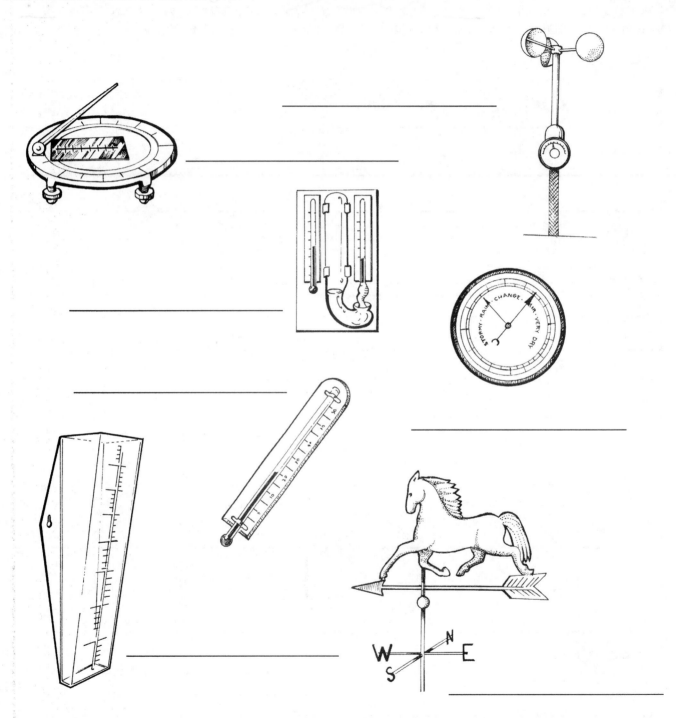

anemometer	hygrometer	rain gauge	weather vane
barometer	nephoscope	thermometer	

Weather Instruments

Identify each instrument and tell what it measures.

A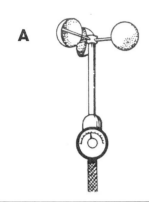

B

C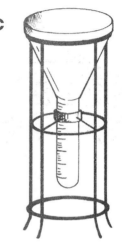

	Weather Instrument	**It Measures...**
A		
B		
C		
D		
E		
F		
G		

D

E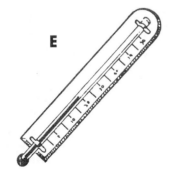

F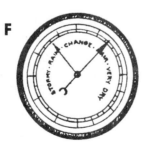

G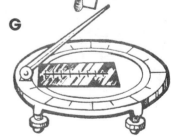

amount of precipitation	hygrometer	thermometer
anemometer	nephoscope	weather vane
atmospheric (air) pressure	rain gauge	wind direction
barometer	relative humidity	wind speed
cloud altitude and direction	temperature	

Weather Crossword

Use your knowledge of weather terms to complete the puzzle.

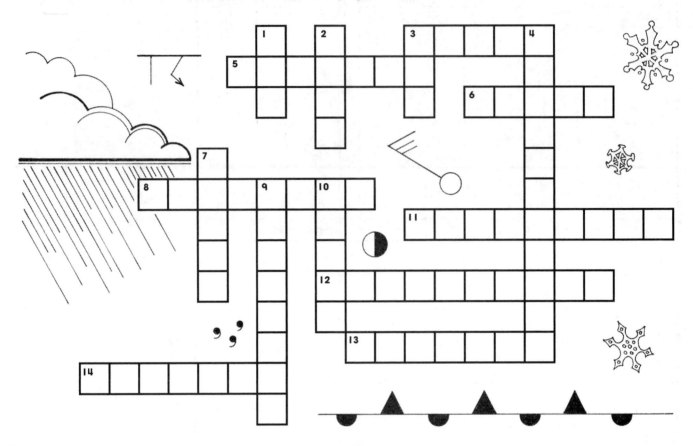

Across

3. Place where two air masses meet
5. Twisting funnel cloud
6. Rain that freezes as it falls
8. Scale used to measure wind speed
11. Measures air pressure
12. Measures wind speed
13. Sound made by rapidly heating and expanding air caused by lightning
14. Layered clouds

Down

1. Cloudy weather occurs in _____-pressure areas.
2. Soft, white crystalline flakes
3. A thick, ground-level mist
4. Measures temperature
7. Precipitation is measured with a rain _____.
9. Prediction of weather in the future
10. Calculates distance of clouds by echoing radio waves

anemometer	front	snow
barometer	gauge	stratus
Beaufort	low	thermometer
fog	radar	thunder
forecast	sleet	tornado

Answer Key

Name_____

A Scientist's Equipment

Scientists use many different kinds of special equipment in a laboratory.

Label each piece of equipment.

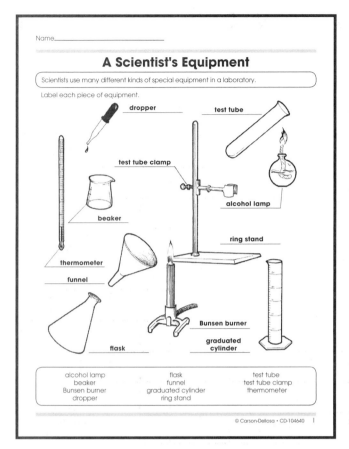

dropper

test tube

test tube clamp

alcohol lamp

beaker

ring stand

thermometer

funnel

Bunsen burner

graduated cylinder

flask

alcohol lamp	flask	test tube
beaker	funnel	test tube clamp
Bunsen burner	graduated cylinder	thermometer
dropper	ring stand	

© Carson-Dellosa • CD-104640   1

Name_____

How Long Is It?

The **meter** is the standard unit of measurement when measuring the length of an object or the distance between two objects.

Use either *kilometer*, *meter*, *centimeter*, or *millimeter* to label the unit used to measure each object.

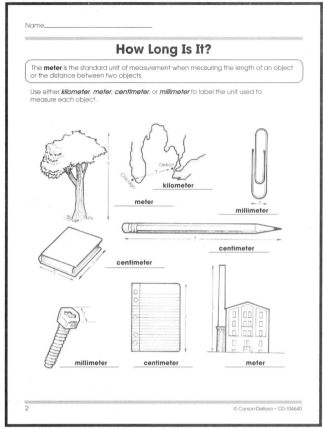

kilometer

meter

millimeter

centimeter

centimeter

centimeter

millimeter

centimeter

meter

2   © Carson-Dellosa • CD-104640

Name_____

The Long and Short of It

Weight, length, area, and volume are properties of matter that scientists can measure. Scientists use the units of grams, meters, and liters to measure these properties.

Write the abbreviation for each unit of measurement.

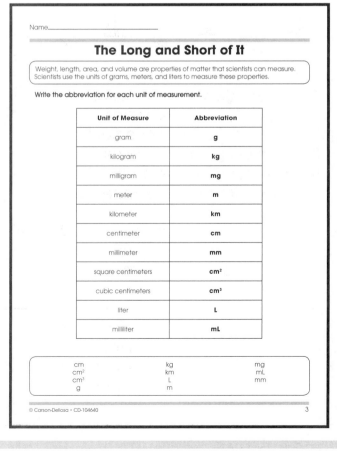

Unit of Measure	Abbreviation
gram	**g**
kilogram	**kg**
milligram	**mg**
meter	**m**
kilometer	**km**
centimeter	**cm**
millimeter	**mm**
square centimeters	**cm²**
cubic centimeters	**cm³**
liter	**L**
milliliter	**mL**

cm	kg	mg
cm²	km	mL
cm³	L	mm
g	m	

© Carson-Dellosa • CD-104640   3

Name_____

Balances

The mass of an object can be measured using a balance. Two common types of balances are the **triple beam balance** and the **double pan balance**.

Name each balance and label the parts. The words in the Word Bank may be used more than once.

Balance: __double pan balance__

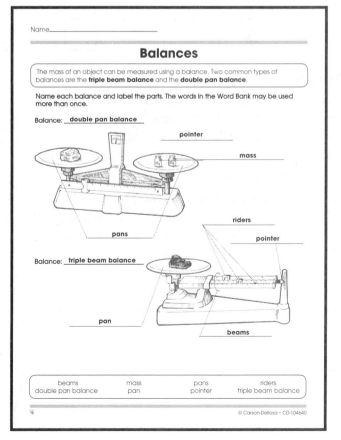

pointer

mass

pans

riders

pointer

Balance: __triple beam balance__

pan

beams

beams	mass	pans	riders
double pan balance	pan	pointer	triple beam balance

4   © Carson-Dellosa • CD-104640

© Carson-Dellosa • CD-104640

Answer Key

Name_____

Reading a Double Pan Balance

To determine the weight of an object using a double pan balance, find the sum of masses needed to balance the two pans. Do this by making the pointer on the balance line up with the indicated line.

Find the mass of each object.

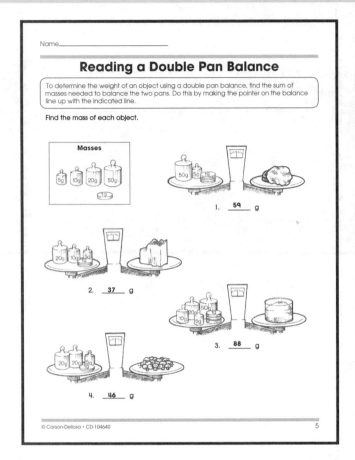

1. __59__ g

2. __37__ g

3. __88__ g

4. __46__ g

Name_____

Reading a Triple Beam Balance

To determine the mass or weight of an object using a triple beam balance, find the sum of the masses shown on the riders.

Find the mass indicated on each triple beam balance.

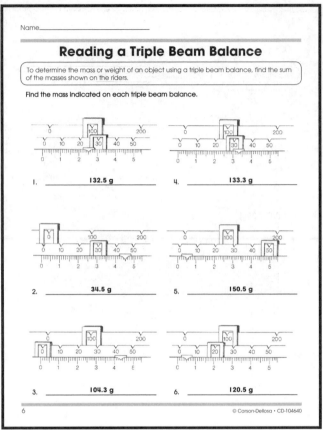

1. __132.5 g__

2. __34.5 g__

3. __104.3 g__

4. __133.3 g__

5. __150.5 g__

6. __120.5 g__

Name_____

Celsius vs. Fahrenheit

The thermometer compares the Celsius and Fahrenheit scales. Label the temperatures on the Celsius and Fahrenheit scales.

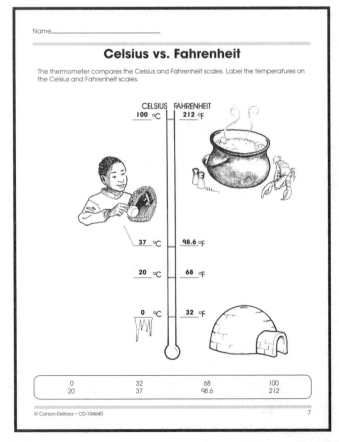

CELSIUS　FAHRENHEIT

100 °C　　**212** °F

37 °C　　**98.6** °F

20 °C　　**68** °F

0 °C　　**32** °F

0	32	68	100
20	37	98.6	212

Name_____

Reading a Graduated Cylinder

Small quantities of a liquid can be measured using a graduated cylinder. Notice how the liquid curves up the side of the cylinder. To get an accurate reading, read the measurement at the bottom of the curve, or **meniscus**.

Read and record each volume.

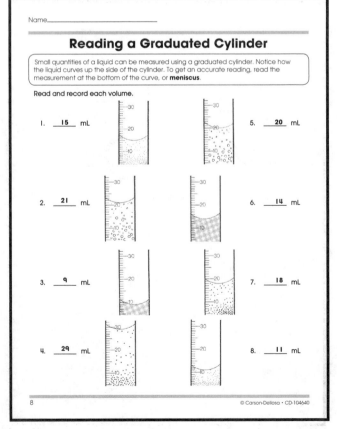

1. __15__ mL

2. __21__ mL

3. __9__ mL

4. __29__ mL

5. __20__ mL

6. __14__ mL

7. __18__ mL

8. __11__ mL

Answer Key

Name_____

Periodic Table of the Elements

The **periodic table** gives a lot of information about each element.

Label the information that the words, numbers, and letters represent for each element.

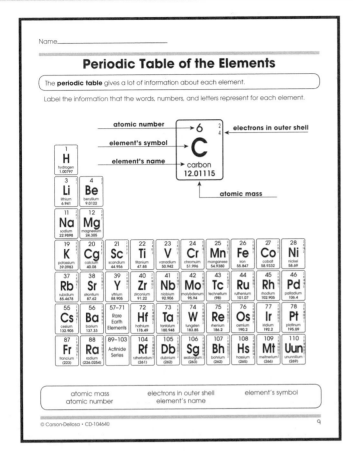

| atomic mass | electrons in outer shell | element's symbol |
| atomic number | element's name | |

Name_____

Chemical Symbols Crossword

Complete the crossword puzzle by matching the symbols to the names of the elements.

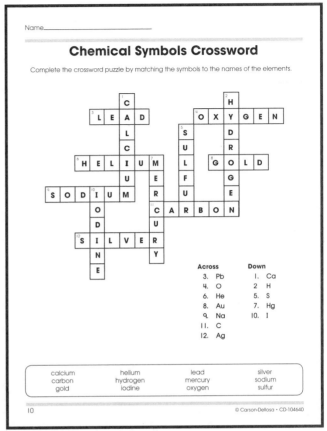

Across
3. Pb
4. O
6. He
8. Au
9. Na
11. C
12. Ag

Down
1. Ca
2. H
5. S
7. Hg
10. I

calcium	helium	lead	silver
carbon	hydrogen	mercury	sodium
gold	iodine	oxygen	sulfur

Name_____

Atoms

All elements are made up of atoms. The **atom** is the smallest particle of an element.

Label the parts of the helium atom.

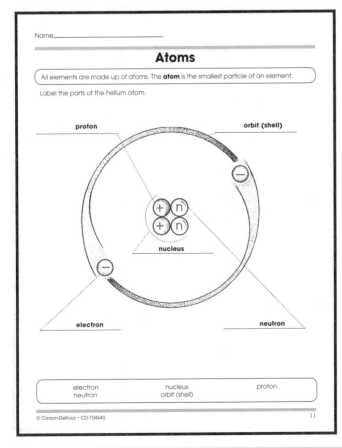

| electron | nucleus | proton |
| neutron | orbit (shell) | |

Name_____

Protons, Neutrons, and Electrons

The **atomic number** of an atom is the number of protons in each atom of that element. Because atoms are electrically neutral, the atomic number is also the number of electrons. The **atomic mass** tells the number of protons and neutrons in an atom. By subtracting the atomic number from the atomic mass, you can find the number of neutrons.

Complete the chart. Round atomic numbers to the nearest whole number.

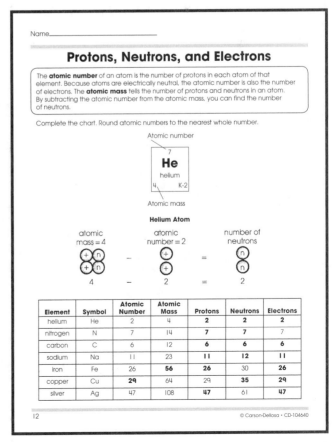

Element	Symbol	Atomic Number	Atomic Mass	Protons	Neutrons	Electrons
helium	He	2	4	**2**	**2**	**2**
nitrogen	N	7	14	**7**	**7**	7
carbon	C	6	12	**6**	**6**	**6**
sodium	Na	11	23	**11**	**12**	**11**
iron	Fe	26	**56**	**26**	30	**26**
copper	Cu	**29**	64	29	**35**	**29**
silver	Ag	47	108	**47**	61	**47**

Answer Key

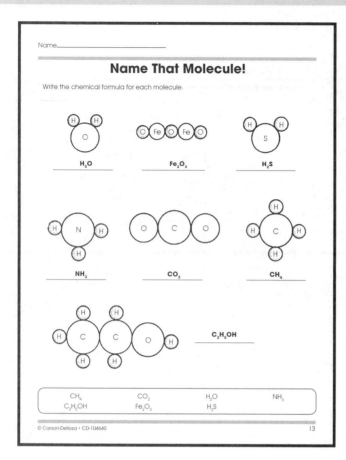

Name That Molecule!

Write the chemical formula for each molecule.

H_2O Fe_2O_3 H_2S

NH_3 CO_2 CH_4

C_2H_5OH

CH_4	CO_2	H_2O	NH_3
C_2H_5OH	Fe_2O_3	H_2S	

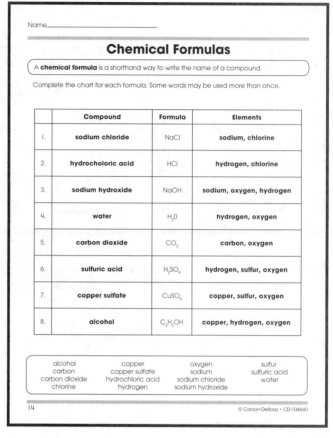

Chemical Formulas

A **chemical formula** is a shorthand way to write the name of a compound.

Complete the chart for each formula. Some words may be used more than once.

	Compound	Formula	Elements
1.	sodium chloride	NaCl	sodium, chlorine
2.	hydrocholoric acid	HCl	hydrogen, chlorine
3.	sodium hydroxide	NaOH	sodium, oxygen, hydrogen
4.	water	H_2O	hydrogen, oxygen
5.	carbon dioxide	CO_2	carbon, oxygen
6.	sulfuric acid	H_2SO_4	hydrogen, sulfur, oxygen
7.	copper sulfate	$CuSO_4$	copper, sulfur, oxygen
8.	alcohol	C_2H_5OH	copper, hydrogen, oxygen

alcohol	copper	oxygen	sulfur
carbon	copper sulfate	sodium	sulfuric acid
carbon dioxide	hydrochloric acid	sodium chloride	water
chlorine	hydrogen	sodium hydroxide	

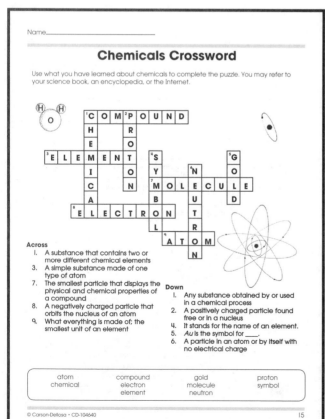

Chemicals Crossword

Use what you have learned about chemicals to complete the puzzle. You may refer to your science book, an encyclopedia, or the Internet.

Across
1. A substance that contains two or more different chemical elements
3. A simple substance made of one type of atom
7. The smallest particle that displays the physical and chemical properties of a compound
8. A negatively charged particle that orbits the nucleus of an atom
9. What everything is made of; the smallest unit of an element

Down
1. Any substance obtained by or used in a chemical process
2. A positively charged particle found free or in a nucleus
4. It stands for the name of an element.
5. *Au* is the symbol for ____.
6. A particle in an atom or by itself with no electrical charge

atom	compound	gold	proton
chemical	electron	molecule	symbol
	element	neutron	

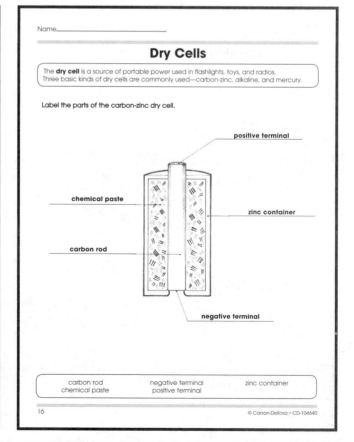

Dry Cells

The **dry cell** is a source of portable power used in flashlights, toys, and radios. Three basic kinds of dry cells are commonly used—carbon-zinc, alkaline, and mercury.

Label the parts of the carbon-zinc dry cell.

positive terminal

chemical paste

zinc container

carbon rod

negative terminal

carbon rod	negative terminal	zinc container
chemical paste	positive terminal	

Answer Key

Name_____

Lightbulbs

Label the parts of the incandescent lightbulb.

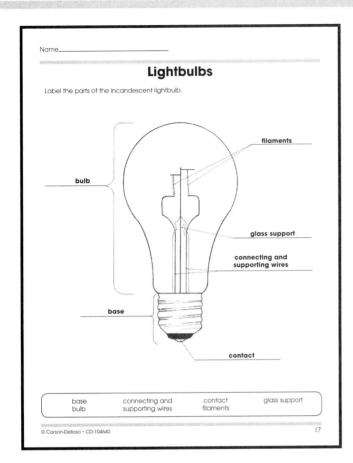

base	connecting and	contact	glass support
bulb	supporting wires	filaments	

Name_____

Circuits and Switches

To be useful, electricity must flow in a circuit. Electric circuits can be illustrated with the help of symbols.

Identify each symbol.

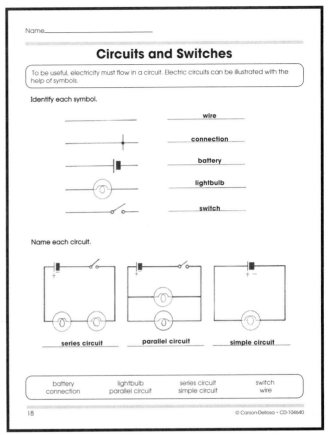

wire

connection

battery

lightbulb

switch

Name each circuit.

series circuit   parallel circuit   simple circuit

battery	lightbulb	series circuit	switch
connection	parallel circuit	simple circuit	wire

Name_____

Drawing Electrical Circuits

There are three types of simple electrical circuits: a **closed circuit**, a **parallel circuit**, and a **series circuit**. Each type can be set up in more than one way.

Draw lines to show where the wires should connect to make each circuit.

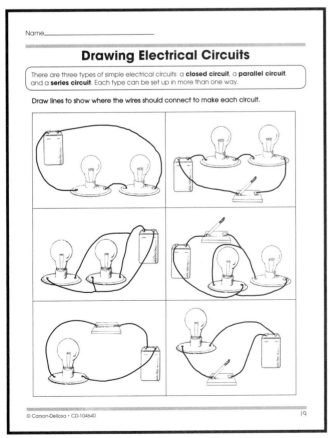

Name_____

Classy Levers

Three classes of levers exist. Levers are identified by the position of the fulcrum and the load.

Label each class of lever and the three lever parts. Some words will be used more than once.

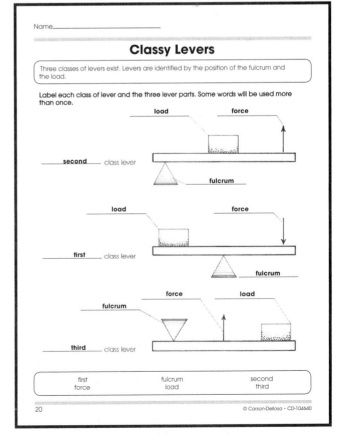

second class lever

first class lever

third class lever

first	fulcrum	second
force	load	third

Answer Key

Name_____

Practical Levers

Under each object, identify the class of the lever as *first, second,* or *third.*

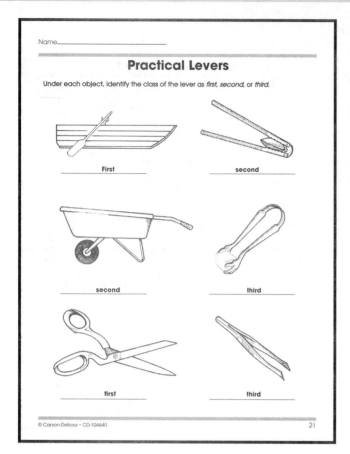

First

second

second

third

first

third

21

Name_____

Special Inclined Planes

Some simple machines are special inclined planes, called wedges and screws. A wedge is an inclined plane that exerts force to widen a space. In a screw, the inclined plane is wrapped around a central point.

Place an **X** on the simple machines that are not special inclined planes. Label the special inclined planes either *screw* or *wedge.*

wedge

wedge

screw

screw

wedge

wedge

screw

22

Name_____

Pedal Power

Most machines use a combination of simple machines to work. For example, your bicycle is a combination of many simple machines. Study the bicycle on this page.

Circle and label as many simple machines as you can find on the bicycle.

Answers will vary, but may include:

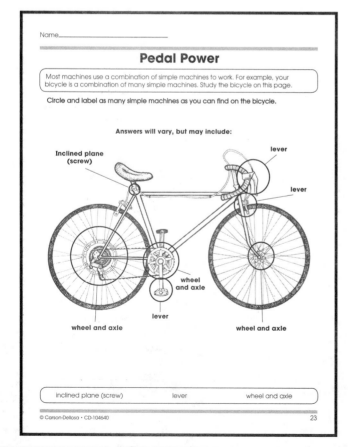

Inclined plane (screw)

lever

lever

wheel and axle

lever

wheel and axle

wheel and axle

| inclined plane (screw) | lever | wheel and axle |

23

Name_____

Compound Machines

Often two or more simple machines are combined to make one machine called a **compound machine**.

Name the simple machines that are combined to make each compound machine.

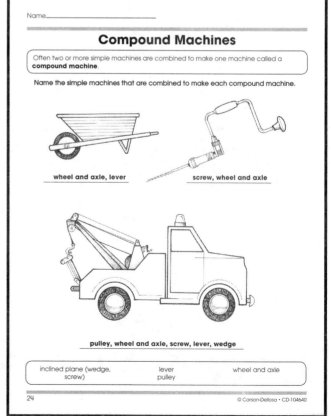

wheel and axle, lever

screw, wheel and axle

pulley, wheel and axle, screw, lever, wedge

| inclined plane (wedge, screw) | lever pulley | wheel and axle |

24

Answer Key

The Seasons

Seasons are important events in Earth's yearly weather cycle. The diagram shows Earth's position in its orbit on four different dates. The seasons are a result of Earth's position in its orbit. Two solstices and two equinoxes occur each year around the same time, though the actual date may vary by a few days.

On the solid lines, label the approximate equinox and solstice dates. On the dotted lines, name the season for the Northern Hemisphere.

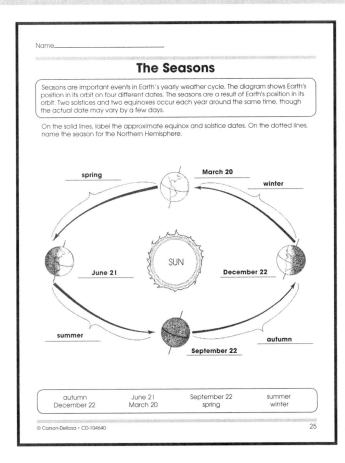

autumn	June 21	September 22	summer
December 22	March 20	spring	winter

Summer and Winter

The illustration shows Earth's position in relation to the sun for summer and winter in the Northern Hemisphere.

Label the seasons for the Northern Hemisphere, and name the imaginary lines of latitude on Earth.

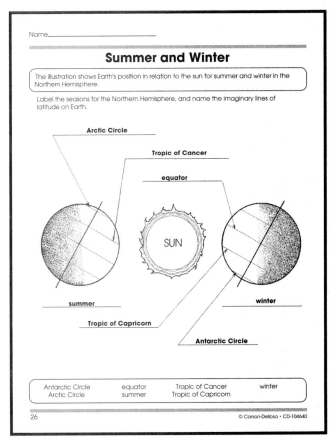

Antarctic Circle	equator	Tropic of Cancer	winter
Arctic Circle	summer	Tropic of Capricorn	

Day and Night

Day and night are the result of Earth's rotation on its axis.

Label the diagram.

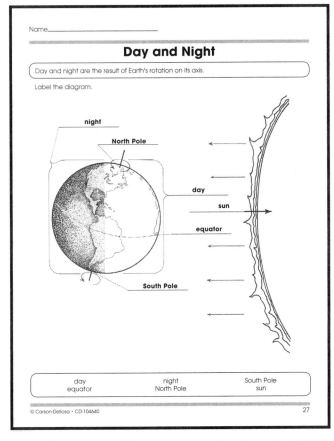

day	night	South Pole
equator	North Pole	sun

High Tide

The ocean tides are the result of gravitational forces from the sun, moon, and rotation of our Earth. When the sun, moon, and Earth line up, the gravitational pull is greatest, causing the highest tides, the **spring tides**. The lowest tides, **neap tides**, occur when the sun, Earth, and moon form right angles.

Label each diagram.

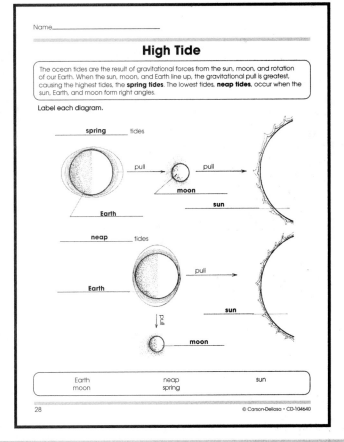

Earth	neap	sun
moon	spring	

Answer Key

Name_____

Space Shadows

When the sun, moon, and Earth are in the proper alignment, either the moon can cast a shadow on Earth, or Earth can cast a shadow on the moon. This is known as an **eclipse**.

Draw the position of the moon and the shadows for both a lunar and solar eclipse. Label the type of eclipse.

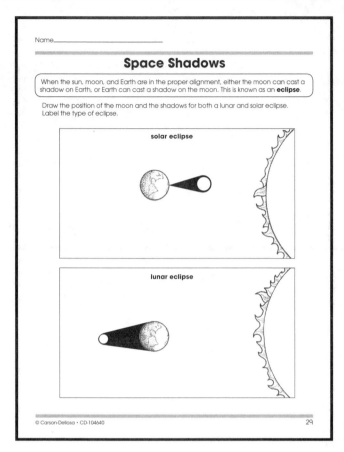

© Carson-Dellosa • CD-104640

29

Name_____

Earth's Shadow

When the sun, Earth, and moon are in a direct line, the moon moves into Earth's shadow, causing a **lunar eclipse**.

Label the orbits and bodies in the diagram.

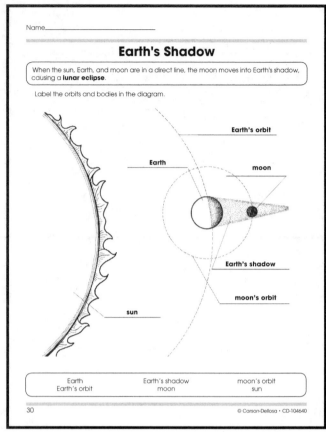

| Earth | Earth's shadow | moon's orbit |
| Earth's orbit | moon | sun |

30

© Carson-Dellosa • CD-104640

Name_____

Moon Shadows

When the new moon is directly between Earth and the sun, an eclipse of the sun occurs. The type of **solar eclipse** that occurs depends on how much sunlight the moon blocks from the view on Earth.

Label the three kinds of solar eclipse. Then, label the moon, sun, and Earth in each diagram.

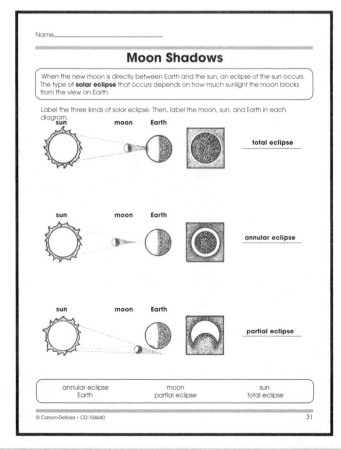

| annular eclipse | moon | sun |
| Earth | partial eclipse | total eclipse |

© Carson-Dellosa • CD-104640

31

Name_____

Changing Faces

As the moon revolves around Earth, we can see different amounts of the moon's lighted side. Study the diagram of the moon's different phases and each phase as it would be seen from Earth.

Label each phase of the moon.

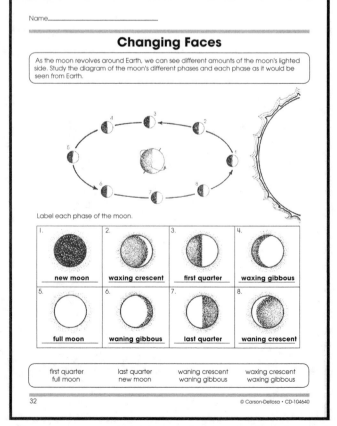

| 1. new moon | 2. waxing crescent | 3. first quarter | 4. waxing gibbous |
| 5. full moon | 6. waning gibbous | 7. last quarter | 8. waning crescent |

| first quarter | last quarter | waning crescent | waxing crescent |
| full moon | new moon | waning gibbous | waxing gibbous |

32

© Carson-Dellosa • CD-104640

Answer Key

Waning and Waxing Moon

Label the different phases of the moon.

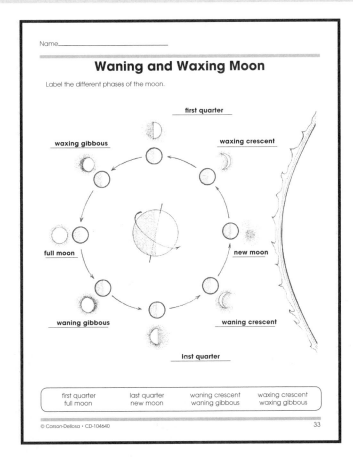

first quarter	last quarter	waning crescent	waxing crescent
full moon	new moon	waning gibbous	waxing gibbous

Planets of the Solar System

All of the planets of the solar system travel around the sun.

Label the planets.

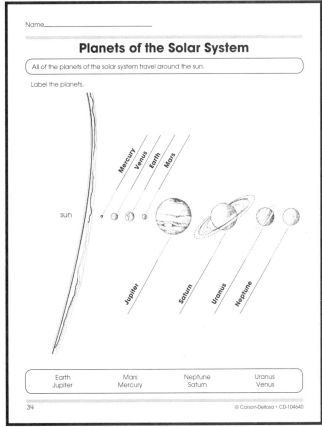

Earth	Mars	Neptune	Uranus
Jupiter	Mercury	Saturn	Venus

The Inner Planets

The planets that are closest to the sun are called the **inner planets**.

Label the inner planets and the sun.

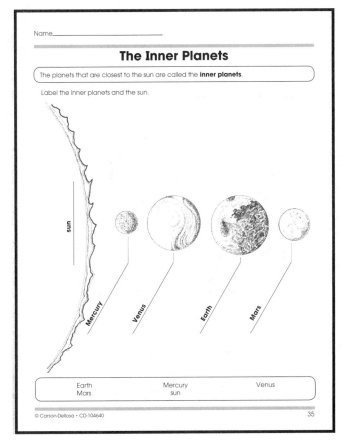

Earth	Mercury	Venus
Mars	sun	

The Outer Planets

The planets that are farthest from the sun are called the **outer planets**.

Label the outer planets.

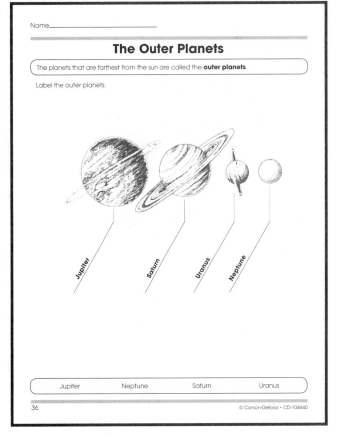

Jupiter	Neptune	Saturn	Uranus

Answer Key

Name

Exporing Our Solar System

Comets, asteroids, and some meteors travel around the sun in our solar system. But the largest objects traveling around the sun are the planets.

Use your science book, an encyclopedia, or an Internet source to complete the chart about the planets of our solar system.

Planet	Position from the Sun	Revolution Time (Length of Year—Earth Days)	Rotation Time	Known Satellites	Distance from the Sun (Miles)
Mercury	1	88	59 days	0	36 million
Venus	2	225	243 days	0	67 million
Earth	3	365	24 hours	1	93 million
Mars	4	687	24 hours	2	142 million
Jupiter	5	4,333	10 hours	67	483 million
Saturn	6	10,759	10 hours	62	888 million
Uranus	7	30,684	17 hours	27	1.78 billion
Neptune	8	60,190	16 hours	14	2.8 billion

Fill in the names of the planets.

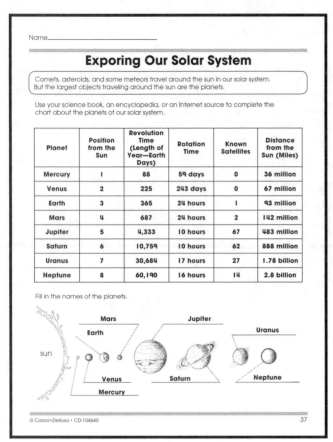

sun — Mercury — Venus — Earth — Mars — Jupiter — Saturn — Uranus — Neptune

---

Name

Planets Crossword

Use what you have learned about the planets of our solar system to complete the puzzle. You may need to refer to your science book, an encyclopedia, or the Internet.

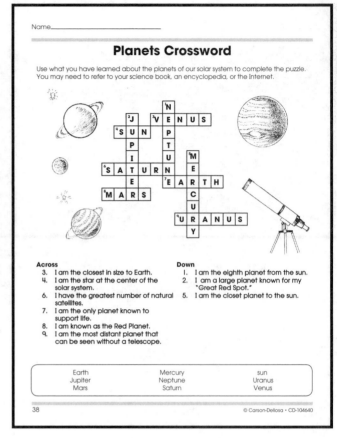

Across
3. I am the closest in size to Earth.
4. I am the star at the center of the solar system.
6. I have the greatest number of natural satellites.
7. I am the only planet known to support life.
8. I am known as the Red Planet.
9. I am the most distant planet that can be seen without a telescope.

Down
1. I am the eighth planet from the sun.
2. I am a large planet known for my "Great Red Spot."
5. I am the closet planet to the sun.

Earth — Mercury — sun
Jupiter — Neptune — Uranus
Mars — Saturn — Venus

Name

Our Closest Star: The Sun

The sun is the closest star to Earth. It is a ball of glowing gases, and life on Earth would not be possible without it.

Label the different layers and features of the sun.

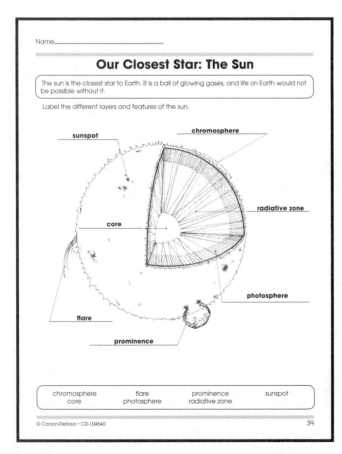

sunspot — chromosphere — radiative zone — core — photosphere — flare — prominence

chromosphere — flare — prominence — sunspot
core — photosphere — radiative zone

Name

Dirty Snowballs

Comets are like "dirty snowballs." They are frozen masses of gas and dust particles. On November 12, 2014, a probe named Philae landed on the first comet. After traveling in space for over 10 years, it will collect data and images to help scientists better understand comets.

Label the parts of the comet.

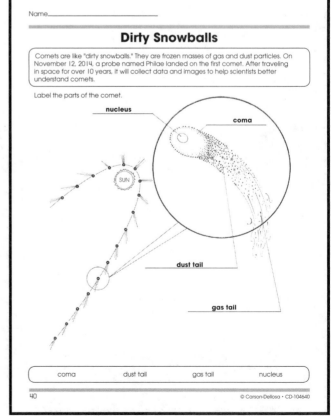

nucleus — coma — SUN — dust tail — gas tail

coma — dust tail — gas tail — nucleus

Answer Key

The Asteroid Belt

Scientists believe that asteroids may be pieces of a planet that was torn apart millions of years ago. Thousands of large asteroids have been tracked, but hundreds of thousands of smaller asteroids are in the asteroid belt.

Label the asteroid belt and the planets.

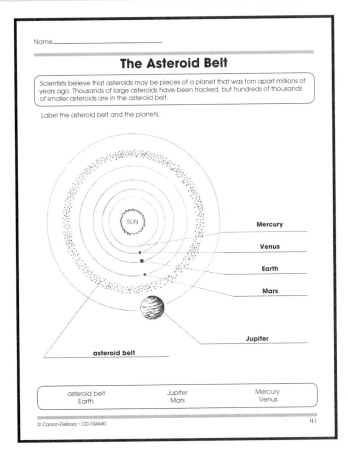

asteroid belt	Jupiter	Mercury
Earth	Mars	Venus

The North Star

As Earth rotates, all the stars in the sky appear to move from east to west. Because Polaris is directly above the North Pole, it does not move, and so it is also called the North Star.

Polaris is found in the constellation Ursa Minor, also called the Little Dipper. The Big Dipper is found in the constellation Ursa Major, also called the Great Bear.

Trace and label the Big Dipper and the Little Dipper. Label Polaris.

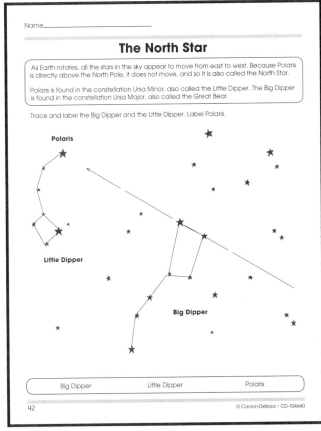

Big Dipper	Little Dipper	Polaris

Pictures in the Night Sky

For thousands of years, people from every culture have gazed into the night sky and imagined groups of stars outlining a picture. These star pictures, called **constellations**, are like giant dot-to-dot puzzles in the night sky.

Name each well-known constellation.

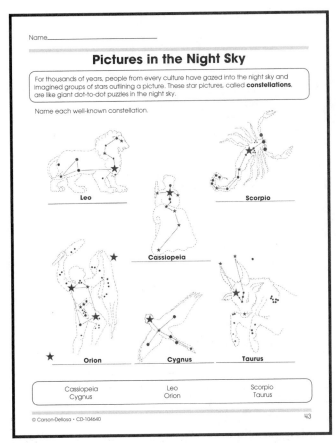

Cassiopeia	Leo	Scorpio
Cygnus	Orion	Taurus

Galaxies

Beyond our galaxy lie billions of other galaxies. The Hubble telescope has enabled us to see into deep space.

Label the shapes of each galaxy.

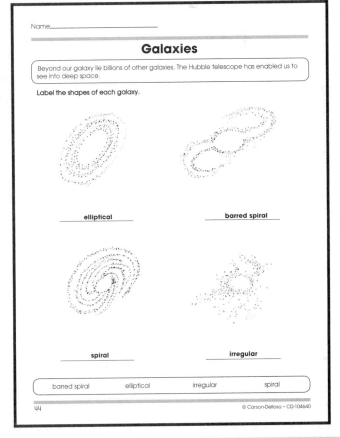

barred spiral	elliptical	irregular	spiral

Answer Key

Radio Telescope

Radio telescopes give us much information about the universe that other types of telescopes can't give. They can detect faint radio waves emitted by extraterrestrial sources.

Label the parts of the radio telescope.

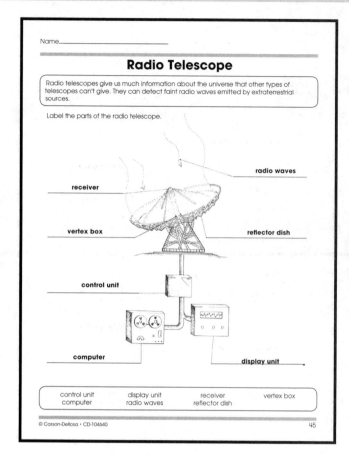

radio waves

receiver

vertex box

reflector dish

control unit

computer

display unit

| control unit | display unit | receiver | vertex box |
| computer | radio waves | reflector dish | |

"Optic Glass"

In 1609, the Italian astronomer, Galilee, was the first person to see the heavenly bodies closer than they really were with his "optic glass," or telescope.

Label the refractor and reflector telescopes and their parts. You may use some words more than once.

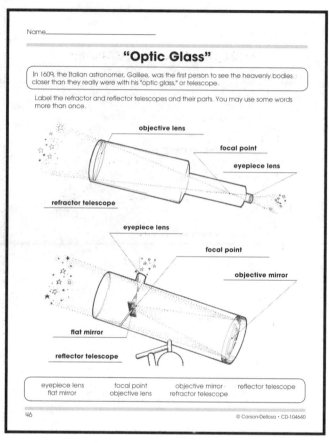

objective lens

focal point

eyepiece lens

refractor telescope

eyepiece lens

focal point

objective mirror

flat mirror

reflector telescope

| eyepiece lens | focal point | objective mirror | reflector telescope |
| flat mirror | objective lens | refractor telescope | |

The Space Shuttle

Label the parts of the space shuttle.

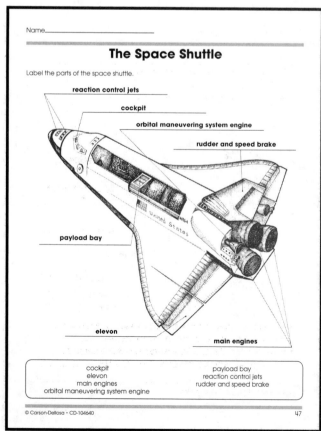

reaction control jets

cockpit

orbital maneuvering system engine

rudder and speed brake

payload bay

elevon

main engines

cockpit	payload bay
elevon	reaction control jets
main engines	rudder and speed brake
orbital maneuvering system engine	

Space Shuttle Launch Site

Label the parts of the space shuttle's launch site.

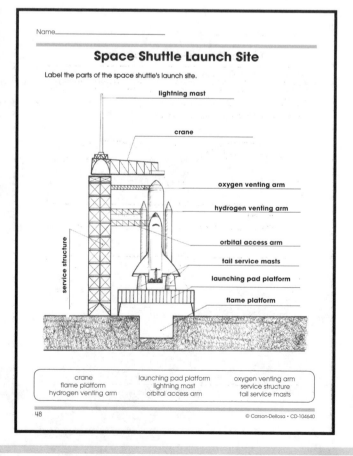

lightning mast

crane

oxygen venting arm

hydrogen venting arm

orbital access arm

tail service masts

launching pad platform

flame platform

service structure

crane	launching pad platform	oxygen venting arm
flame platform	lightning mast	service structure
hydrogen venting arm	orbital access arm	tail service masts

Answer Key

Name_____

The Flight of the Space Shuttle

Label the different phases of the space shuttle's mission.

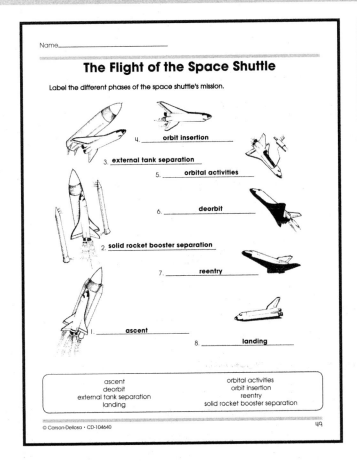

4. **orbit insertion**

3. **external tank separation**

5. **orbital activities**

6. **deorbit**

2. **solid rocket booster separation**

7. **reentry**

1. **ascent**

8. **landing**

ascent	orbital activities
deorbit	orbit insertion
external tank separation	reentry
landing	solid rocket booster separation

Name_____

Hemispheres

Earth is a giant sphere. When Earth is divided into two equal parts, each part is called a **hemisphere**.

Label the four hemispheres.

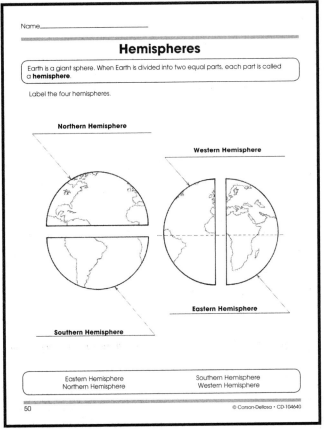

Northern Hemisphere

Western Hemisphere

Eastern Hemisphere

Southern Hemisphere

Eastern Hemisphere	Southern Hemisphere
Northern Hemisphere	Western Hemisphere

Name_____

More Than One Hemisphere

You live in more than one hemisphere. Although it is impossible to live in the Northern and Southern Hemispheres or the Eastern and Western Hemispheres at the same time, it is possible to live in the Northern and Eastern, Northern and Western, Southern and Eastern, or Southern and Western Hemispheres.

Label the two hemispheres pictured in each image.

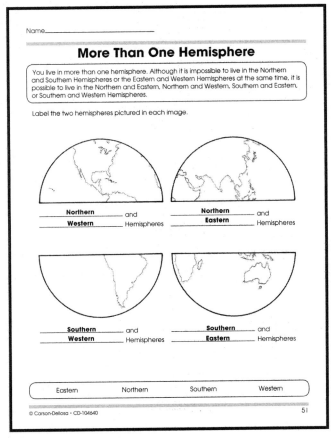

Northern and **Western** Hemispheres

Northern and **Eastern** Hemispheres

Southern and **Western** Hemispheres

Southern and **Eastern** Hemispheres

Eastern	Northern	Southern	Western

Name_____

Map Features

Everyone from the weather forecaster to a family on vacation finds maps as very valuable tools. But, they are useful only if you know how to use their many features.

Label the parts of the map. Then, explain the purpose of each.

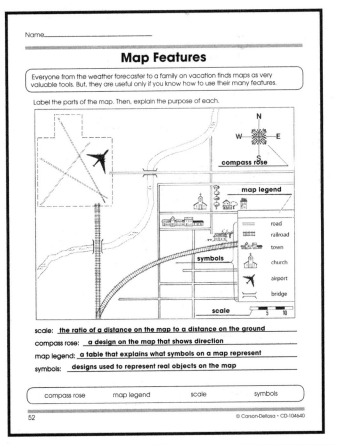

compass rose

map legend

road
railroad
town
symbols
church
airport
bridge

scale

scale: the ratio of a distance on the map to a distance on the ground

compass rose: a design on the map that shows direction

map legend: a table that explains what symbols on a map represent

symbols: designs used to represent real objects on the map

compass rose	map legend	scale	symbols

Answer Key

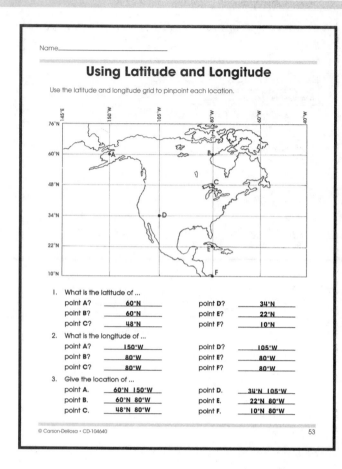
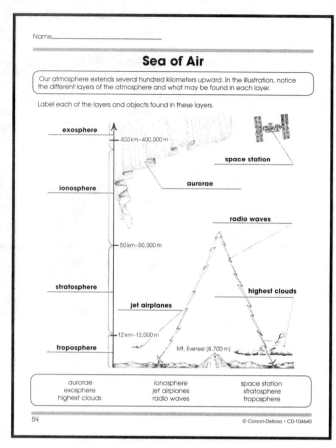
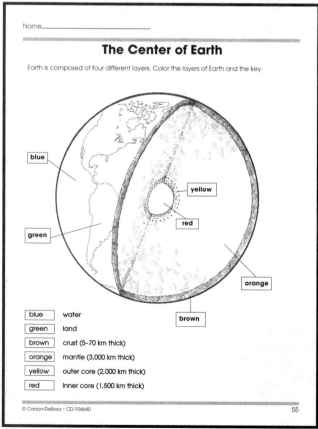
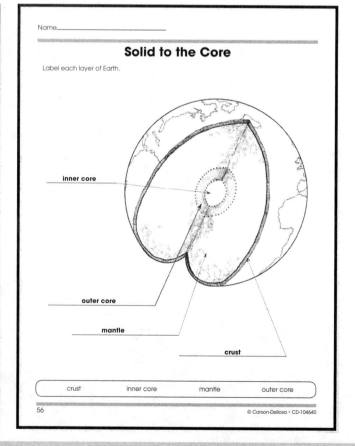

Answer Key

The Rock Cycle

With the help of heat, pressure, and weathering, one type of rock can be changed into a new type of rock. For example, beautiful marble is formed from limestone, and slate comes from shale and clay. The changing of rocks is an ongoing cycle. No true beginning exists, but it might be easier to understand by beginning with magma.

Complete the rock cycle diagram.

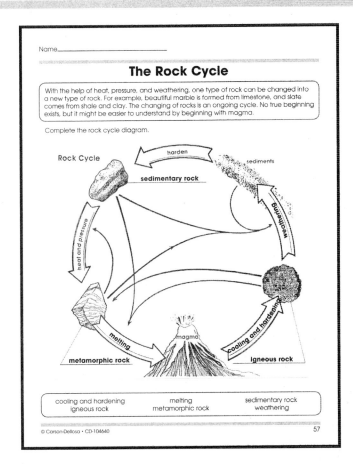

| cooling and hardening | melting | sedimentary rock |
| igneous rock | metamorphic rock | weathering |

57

Soil Profile

Examine the solid profile pictured. Identify the layer(s) where each of the following are found.

- __A__ live animals
- __B,C__ rock
- __B__ minerals
- __A__ live plants
- __A__ organic matter
- __A__ top layer
- __B__ middle layer
- __C__ lowest layer
- __A__ topsoil
- __B__ subsoil
- __A, B__ tree roots
- __C__ boulders

58

Making Crystals

Crystals come in a wide variety of shapes, colors, and sizes. People have always been fascinated by their incredible beauty.

Cut out each of the crystal patterns on the solid line. Then, fold along the dotted lines. Tape the sides together. Match the common crystal shapes drawn here with the ones you have created.

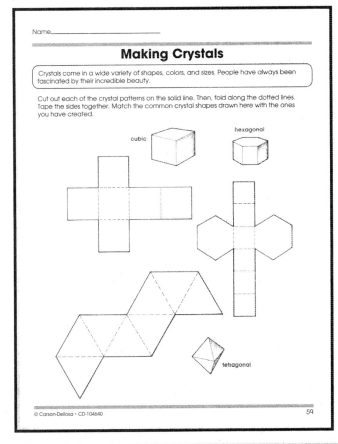

59

Mohs' Hardness Scale

One of the most useful properties applied in the identification of a mineral is its hardness. The **Mohs' hardness scale** measures a mineral's hardness by a simple scratch test.

Name the mineral that belongs in each step of the Mohs' hardness scale chart.

Mohs' Hardness Scale		
Hardness	**Mineral**	**Common Tests**
1	**talc**	Fingernail will scratch it.
2	**gypsum**	
3	**calcite**	Fingernail will not scratch it; a copper penny will.
4	**fluorite**	Knife blade or window glass will scratch it.
5	**apatite**	
6	feldspar/orthoclase	Will scratch a steel knife or window glass.
7	**quartz**	
8	**topaz**	
9	**corundum**	
10	**diamond**	Will scratch all common materials.

apatite	corundum	fluorite	talc
calcite	diamond	gypsum	topaz
	feldspar/orthoclase	quartz	

60

Answer Key

Name That Mineral

One can identify minerals by carefully observing their physical characteristics. Some of these characteristics are:
Hardness—This is determined with a scratch test.
Color—Color depends on the substances that make up the crystals. It varies greatly.
Luster—This refers to how light reflects off the mineral.

Find the unknown minerals and fill in the chart.

Hardness Scale

Hardness	Mineral	Common Tests
1	talc	Fingernail will scratch it.
2	gypsum, kaolinite	
3	mica, calcite	A copper penny will scratch it.
4	fluorite	Knife blade or window glass will scratch it.
5	apatite, hornblende	
6	feldspar	Will scratch a steel knife or window glass.
7	quartz	
8	topaz	
9	corundum	
10	diamond	Will scratch all common materials.

Color	Mineral
White	quartz, feldspar, calcite, kaolinite, talc
Yellow	quartz, kaolinite
Black	hornblende, mica
Gray	feldspar, gypsum
Colorless	quartz, calcite, gypsum

Luster	Mineral
Glassy	quartz, feldspar, hornblende
Pearly	mica, gypsum, talc
Dull	kaolinite

Hardness	Color	Luster	Mineral
It will scratch a steel knife or window glass.	yellow	glassy	**quartz**
It will scratch a steel knife or window glass.	gray	glassy	**feldspar**
A copper penny will scratch it.	black	pearly	**mica**
A fingernail will scratch it.	white	pearly	**talc**
A knife blade or window glass will scratch it.	black	glassy	**hornblende**

Classy Rocks

Three main groups of rock exist: **igneous** rock, **metamorphic** rock, and **sedimentary** rock. Each of the pictured rocks belongs to one of these groups.

Complete the definitions. Then, identify which group each rock belongs to.

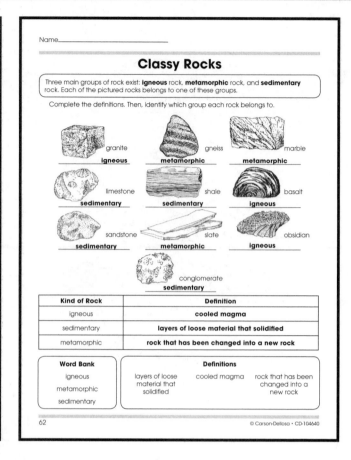

granite — **igneous**
gneiss — **metamorphic**
marble — **metamorphic**
limestone — **sedimentary**
shale — **sedimentary**
basalt — **igneous**
sandstone — **sedimentary**
slate — **metamorphic**
obsidian — **igneous**
conglomerate — **sedimentary**

Kind of Rock	Definition
igneous	**cooled magma**
sedimentary	**layers of loose material that solidified**
metamorphic	**rock that has been changed into a new rock**

Word Bank	Definitions		
igneous	layers of loose material that solidified	cooled magma	rock that has been changed into a new rock
metamorphic			
sedimentary			

Rocks and Minerals Crossword

Use your knowledge of rocks and minerals to complete the puzzle.

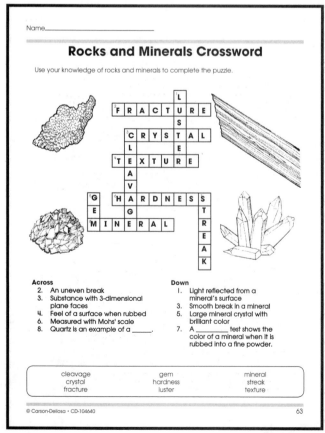

Across
2. An uneven break
3. Substance with 3-dimensional plane faces
4. Feel of a surface when rubbed
6. Measured with Mohs' scale
8. Quartz is an example of a _____.

Down
1. Light reflected from a mineral's surface
3. Smooth break in a mineral
5. Large mineral crystal with brilliant color
7. A _____ test shows the color of a mineral when it is rubbed into a fine powder.

cleavage	gem	mineral
crystal	hardness	streak
fracture	luster	texture

Whose Fault Is It?

A crack in Earth's bedrock is called a **fault**. Two types of faults exist: the **strike-slip fault** and the **normal**, or **dip-slip fault**.

California is known for the San Andreas Fault. Draw the San Andreas Fault on the map of California. Then, label the two different kinds of faults.

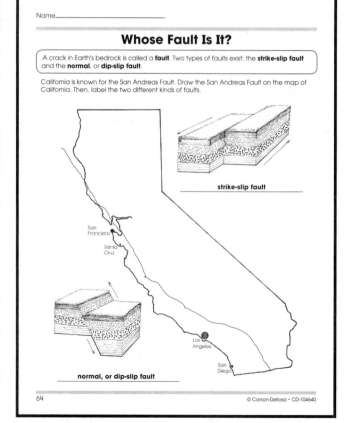

strike-slip fault

normal, or dip-slip fault

Answer Key

Name_____

Drifting Continents

About 250 million years ago, one continent existed, called Pangaea (Figure A). By 45 million years ago, the land mass split into seven land masses (Figure B).

Label the land masses in Figure B.

Figure A

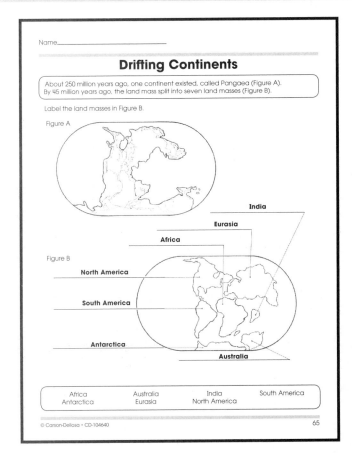

Figure B

Africa	Australia	India	South America
Antarctica	Eurasia	North America	

Name_____

Earth's Moving Plates

Earth's crust is made of rigid plates that are always moving. The boundaries of some plates are along the edges of the continents, while others are in the middle of the ocean. The map on this page shows the major plates near North and South America.

Using an encyclopedia, a textbook, or the Internet, label the eight plates.

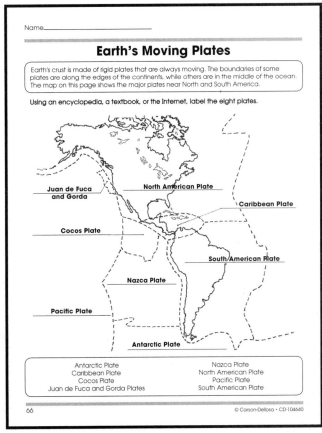

Antarctic Plate	Nazca Plate
Caribbean Plate	North American Plate
Cocos Plate	Pacific Plate
Juan de Fuca and Gorda Plates	South American Plate

Name_____

"Broken Plates"

Below are puzzle pieces of Earth's seven major plates. Cut out the plates and glue them on a separate sheet of paper. Label the plates.

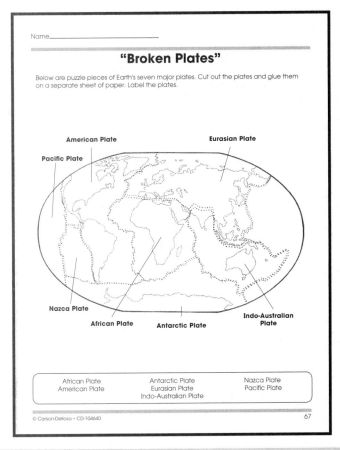

African Plate	Antarctic Plate	Nazca Plate
American Plate	Eurasian Plate	Pacific Plate
	Indo-Australian Plate	

Name_____

Bending Earth's Crust

According to the theory of plate tectonics, Earth's crust is broken into about twenty **plates**. These plates are slowly moving. The edges of some plates are moving toward each other. A **trench** is formed when one plate bends and dives under another. The diving edge then descends into Earth's hot **mantle** and starts melting into magma. The **magma** can then rise and break through Earth's crust bursting out of a **volcano**. The edge of the overriding plate crumples, resulting in a mountain range.

Label the diagram.

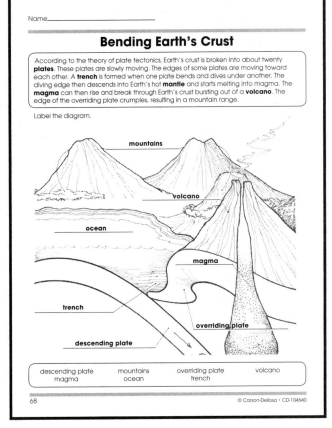

descending plate	mountains	overriding plate	volcano
magma	ocean	trench	

Answer Key

Volcanoes

Name_____

Label the parts of the volcano.

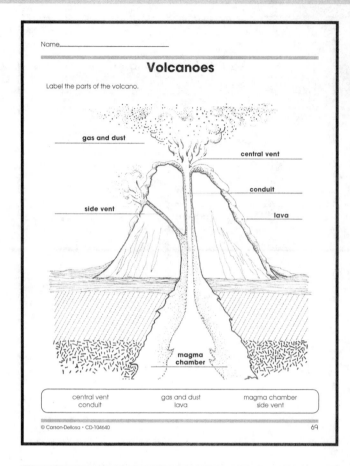

- gas and dust
- central vent
- conduit
- side vent
- lava
- magma chamber

central vent	gas and dust	magma chamber
conduit	lava	side vent

69

Ring of Fire

Name_____

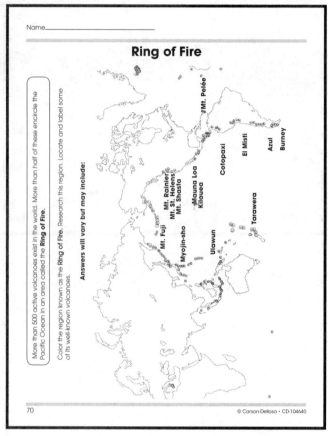

More than 500 active volcanoes exist in the world. More than half of these encircle the Pacific Ocean in an area called the **Ring of Fire**.

Color the region known as the **Ring of Fire**. Research this region. Locate and label some of its well-known volcanoes.

Answers will vary but may include:

- Mt. Pelée
- El Misti
- Azul
- Burney
- Cotopaxi
- Mt. Rainier
- Mt. St. Helens
- Mt. Shasta
- Mauna Loa
- Kilauea
- Tarawera
- Mt. Fuji
- Myojin-sho
- Ulawun

70

Volcanic Cones

Name_____

Volcanic cones can be classified by their shapes. Label the three different kinds of volcanic cones and their parts. Some words may be used more than once.

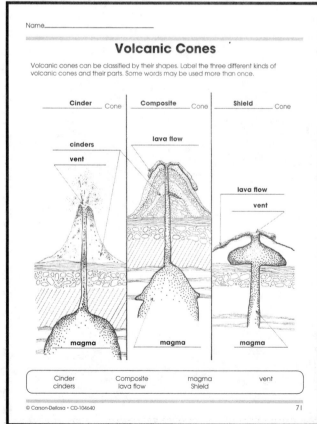

- Cinder Cone
- Composite Cone
- Shield Cone
- cinders
- vent
- lava flow
- lava flow
- vent
- magma
- magma
- magma

Cinder	Composite	magma	vent
cinders	lava flow	Shield	

71

Forming Igneous Rock

Name_____

Igneous rock is one of the three major types of rock, formed by the hardening of molten rock (magma). Magma does not always reach Earth's surface as erupting lava. It can form other igneous rock structures underground.

Label the igneous rock structures.

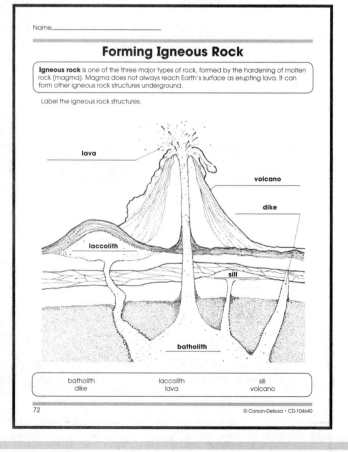

- lava
- volcano
- dike
- laccolith
- sill
- batholith

batholith	laccolith	sill
dike	lava	volcano

72

Answer Key

Drilling for Oil

Most oil is found thousands of feet beneath the surface of the earth. Trapped beneath layers of nonporous rock, such as shale, oil cannot reach the surface. Pockets of natural gas will often form where oil is. Oil companies drill for oil using large drills that grind through layers of soil and bedrock.

The illustration shows one example of how oil can be found. Label the illustration.

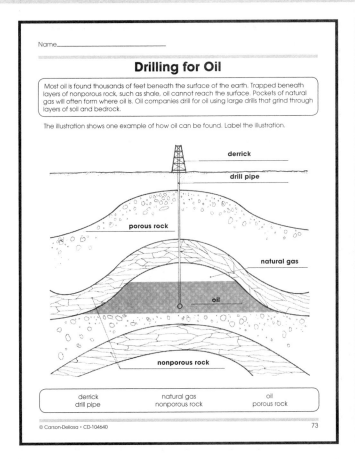

- derrick
- drill pipe
- porous rock
- natural gas
- oil
- nonporous rock

| derrick | natural gas | oil |
| drill pipe | nonporous rock | porous rock |

Coral Reefs

Three types of coral reefs are pictured. Label each type of coral reef and the feature that is enclosed by the reef. Then, number the steps in the formation of an atoll.

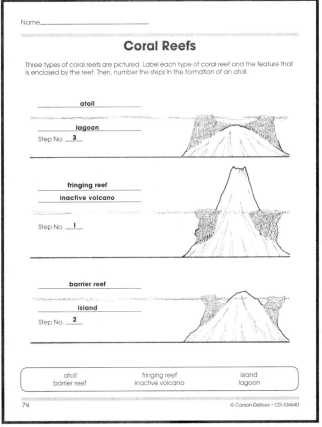

- atoll
- lagoon
- Step No. __3__

- fringing reef
- inactive volcano
- Step No. __1__

- barrier reef
- island
- Step No. __2__

| atoll | fringing reef | island |
| barrier reef | inactive volcano | lagoon |

Groundwater at Work

Groundwater is water located beneath the surface in pore spaces, fractures, and open formations. People remove groundwater with wells.

Label each diagram.

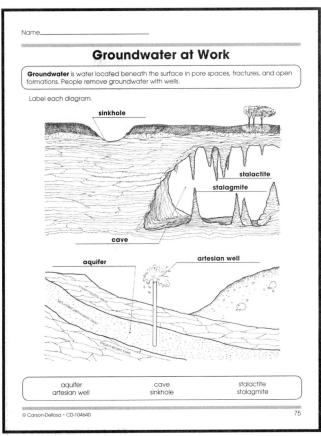

- sinkhole
- stalactite
- stalagmite
- cave
- aquifer
- artesian well

| aquifer | cave | stalactite |
| artesian well | sinkhole | stalagmite |

The Ocean Floor

Label the features of the ocean floor.

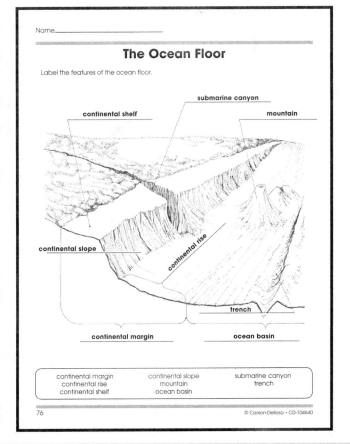

- continental shelf
- submarine canyon
- mountain
- continental slope
- continental rise
- trench
- continental margin
- ocean basin

continental margin	continental slope	submarine canyon
continental rise	mountain	trench
continental shelf	ocean basin	

Answer Key

Ocean Currents

Water moves within the oceans in streams called **currents**. Several major currents are always present in the world's oceans.

Label the ocean currents pictured on the map.

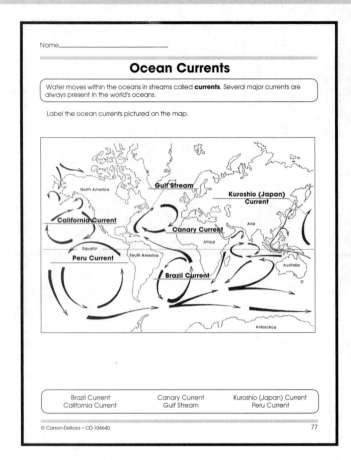

Brazil Current	Canary Current	Kuroshio (Japan) Current
California Current	Gulf Stream	Peru Current

Landform Regions of the United States

The continental United States can be divided into several major landform regions. Label each region.

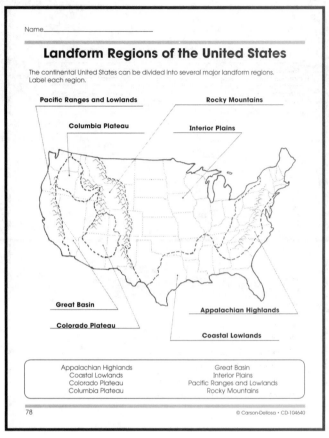

Appalachian Highlands	Great Basin
Coastal Lowlands	Interior Plains
Colorado Plateau	Pacific Ranges and Lowlands
Columbia Plateau	Rocky Mountains

Topographic Maps

A **topographic map** uses contour lines to show the elevation and slope of hills, valleys, and other natural features.

Label the various land features and elements of the topographic map.

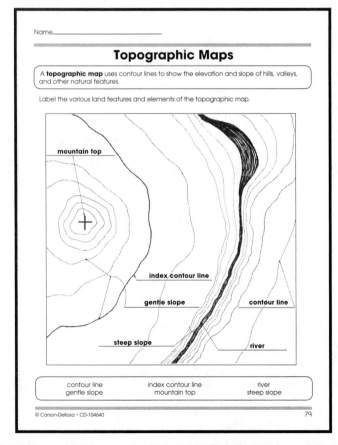

contour line	index contour line	river
gentle slope	mountain top	steep slope

Benchmark to Benchmark

Use the benchmarks on the map to help you draw the contour lines. The contour lines should be drawn at 20-foot intervals.

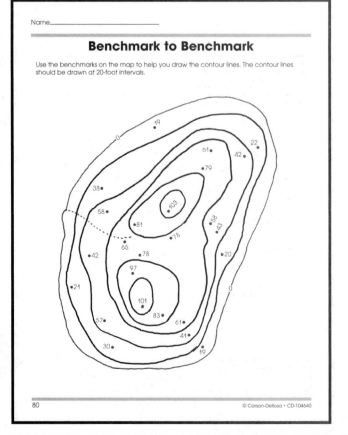

Answer Key

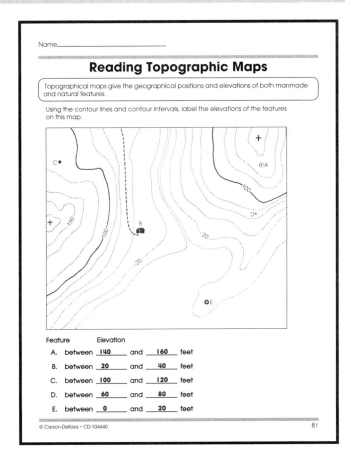
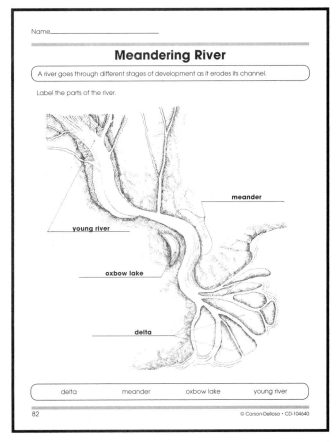
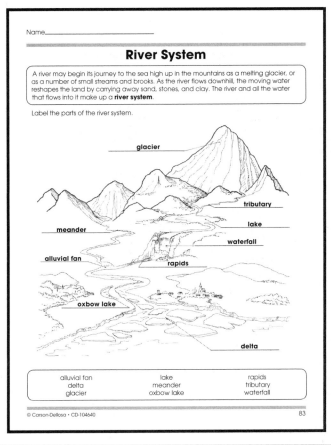
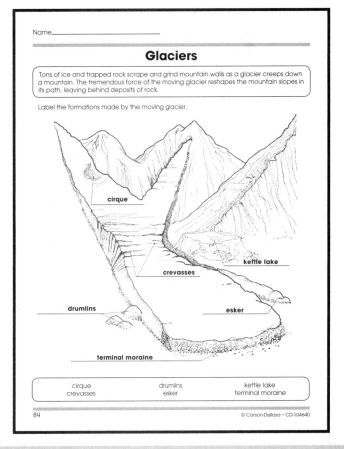

Answer Key

You're All Wet

It's a wet day! The symbols on the weather map show eight different forms of precipitation occuring around the country. Label each form of precipitation.

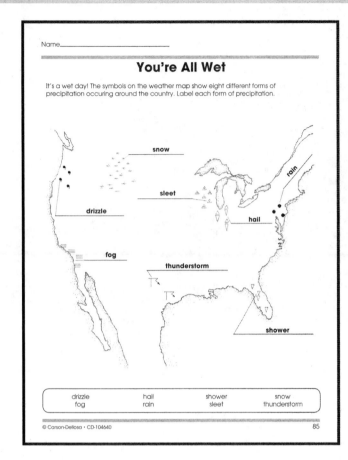

drizzle	hail	shower	snow
fog	rain	sleet	thunderstorm

85

Gentle Breezes

On the chart, fill in the wind speed and wind direction for each city.

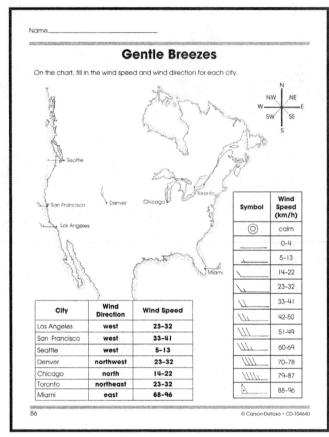

Symbol	Wind Speed (km/h)
◎	calm
	0–4
	5–13
	14–22
	23–32
	33–41
	42–50
	51–49
	60–69
	70–78
	79–87
	88–96

City	Wind Direction	Wind Speed
Los Angeles	west	23–32
San Francisco	west	33–41
Seattle	west	5–13
Denver	northwest	23–32
Chicago	north	14–22
Toronto	northeast	23–32
Miami	east	88–96

86

Weather Map Symbols

Weather maps provide data from which meteorologists prepare weather forecasts. To accurately read a weather map, you must be able to understand the weather map symbols.

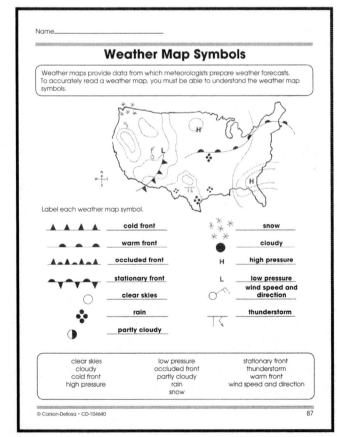

Label each weather map symbol.

cold front	snow
warm front	cloudy
occluded front	high pressure
stationary front	low pressure
clear skies	wind speed and direction
rain	thunderstorm
partly cloudy	

clear skies	low pressure	stationary front
cloudy	occluded front	thunderstorm
cold front	partly cloudy	warm front
high pressure	rain	wind speed and direction
	snow	

87

Using a Weather Map

Weather maps show the recorded weather conditions over a large geographic area.

Use the map along with what you have learned about weather symbols to complete the chart.

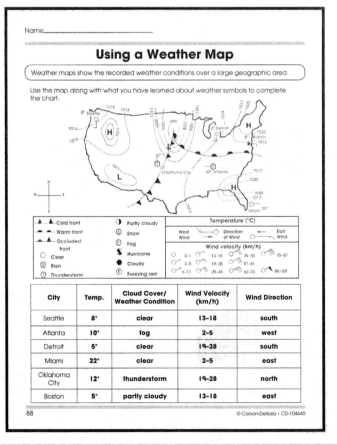

City	Temp.	Cloud Cover/ Weather Condition	Wind Velocity (km/h)	Wind Direction
Seattle	8°	clear	13–18	south
Atlanta	10°	fog	2–5	west
Detroit	5°	clear	19–28	south
Miami	22°	clear	2–5	east
Oklahoma City	12°	thunderstorm	19–28	north
Boston	5°	partly cloudy	13–18	east

88

Answer Key

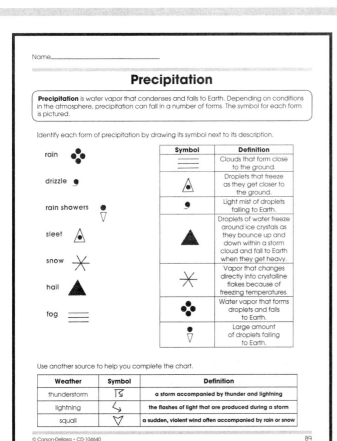

Precipitation

Precipitation is water vapor that condenses and falls to Earth. Depending on conditions in the atmosphere, precipitation can fall in a number of forms. The symbol for each form is pictured.

Identify each form of precipitation by drawing its symbol next to its description.

rain ⦿

drizzle ,

rain showers ⦿▽

sleet △

snow ✳

hail ▲

fog ☰

Symbol	Definition
☰	Clouds that form close to the ground.
△	Droplets that freeze as they get closer to the ground.
,	Light mist of droplets falling to Earth.
▲	Droplets of water freeze around ice crystals as they bounce up and down within a storm cloud and fall to Earth when they get heavy.
✳	Vapor that changes directly into crystalline flakes because of freezing temperatures.
⦿	Water vapor that forms droplets and falls to Earth.
⦿▽	Large amount of droplets falling to Earth.

Use another source to help you complete the chart.

Weather	Symbol	Definition
thunderstorm	⚡	a storm accompanied by thunder and lightning
lightning	↯	the flashes of light that are produced during a storm
squall	▽	a sudden, violent wind often accompanied by rain or snow

© Carson-Dellosa • CD-104640   89

Moving Weather Systems

A careful study of daily weather maps will show that weather systems are constantly on the move. You will need four copies of this page. Use a new sheet every day for three days to copy that day's weather pattern (frontal systems, pressure cells, and precipitation) from your newspaper or the Internet. Study the movement of the pattern. Then, draw a weather pattern predicting where the weather systems will move on the next day.

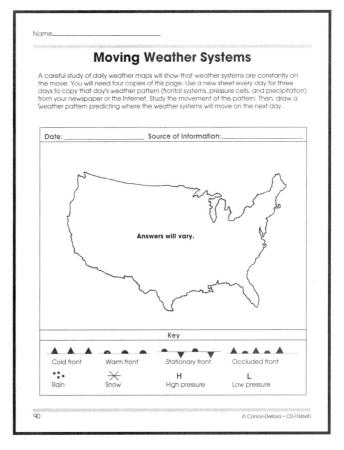

Date: _____   Source of Information: _____

Answers will vary.

Key

▲▲▲ Cold front   ◗◗◗ Warm front   ▲◗▲◗ Stationary front   ▲◗▲ Occluded front

⦿ Rain   ✳ Snow   H High pressure   L Low pressure

90   © Carson-Dellosa • CD-104640

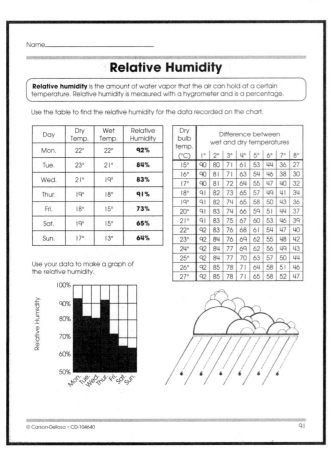

Relative Humidity

Relative humidity is the amount of water vapor that the air can hold at a certain temperature. Relative humidity is measured with a hygrometer and is a percentage.

Use the table to find the relative humidity for the data recorded on the chart.

Day	Dry Temp.	Wet Temp.	Relative Humidity
Mon.	22°	22°	**92%**
Tue.	23°	21°	**84%**
Wed.	21°	19°	**83%**
Thur.	19°	18°	**91%**
Fri.	18°	15°	**73%**
Sat.	19°	15°	**65%**
Sun.	17°	13°	**64%**

Dry bulb temp. (°C)	Difference between wet and dry temperatures							
	1°	2°	3°	4°	5°	6°	7°	8°
15°	90	80	71	61	53	44	36	27
16°	90	81	71	63	54	46	38	30
17°	90	81	72	64	55	47	40	32
18°	91	82	73	65	57	49	41	34
19°	91	82	74	65	58	50	43	36
20°	91	83	74	66	59	51	44	37
21°	91	83	75	67	60	53	46	39
22°	92	83	76	68	61	54	47	40
23°	92	84	76	69	62	55	48	42
24°	92	84	77	69	62	56	49	43
25°	92	84	77	70	63	57	50	44
26°	92	85	78	71	64	58	51	46
27°	92	85	78	71	65	58	52	47

Use your data to make a graph of the relative humidity.

Relative Humidity graph: 100%, 90%, 80%, 70%, 60%, 50% — Mon. Tue. Wed. Thur. Fri. Sat. Sun.

© Carson-Dellosa • CD-104640   91

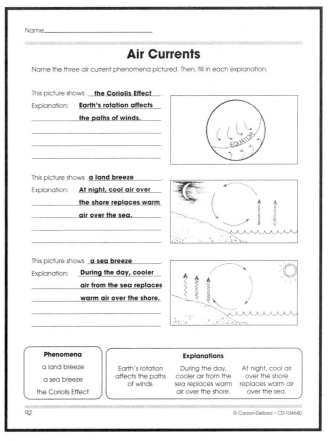

Air Currents

Name the three air current phenomena pictured. Then, fill in each explanation.

This picture shows ___**the Coriolis Effect**___

Explanation: **Earth's rotation affects the paths of winds.**

This picture shows **a land breeze**

Explanation: **At night, cool air over the shore replaces warm air over the sea.**

This picture shows **a sea breeze**

Explanation: **During the day, cooler air from the sea replaces warm air over the shore.**

Phenomena
a land breeze
a sea breeze
the Coriolis Effect

Explanations		
Earth's rotation affects the paths of winds.	During the day, cooler air from the sea replaces warm air over the shore.	At night, cool air over the shore replaces warm air over the sea.

92   © Carson-Dellosa • CD-104640

Answer Key

Name_____

The Water Cycle

The continuous circulation of water on Earth from the oceans, to the air, and to the land is called the **water cycle**.

Label the three major steps in the water cycle and explain how the water cycle works.

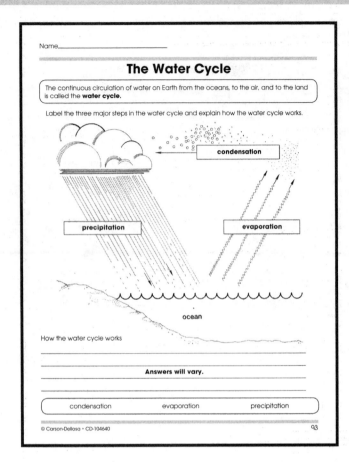

condensation

precipitation   evaporation

ocean

How the water cycle works

_____

Answers will vary.

_____

condensation	evaporation	precipitation

Name_____

What's Up Front?

A **front** is where two air masses meet or converge. Changes in the weather take place along a front.

Label the two fronts and the kinds of air masses shown.

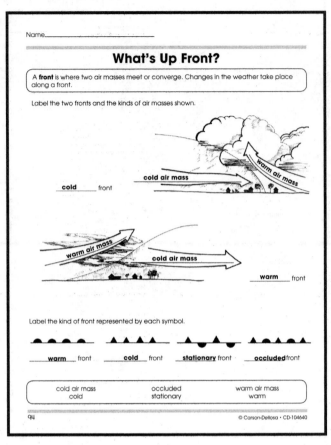

cold air mass

cold front

warm air mass   cold air mass

warm front

Label the kind of front represented by each symbol.

warm front   **cold** front   **stationary** front   **occluded** front

cold air mass	occluded	warm air mass
cold	stationary	warm

Name_____

A Cold Front

This illustration shows a front between two air masses. The cooler air mass is replacing the warmer air mass.

Label the cloud types associated with the cold front.

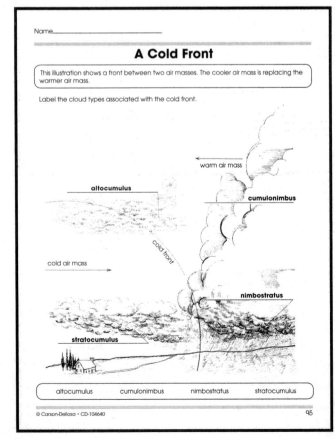

warm air mass

altocumulus   **cumulonimbus**

cold air mass

nimbostratus

stratocumulus

altocumulus	cumulonimbus	nimbostratus	stratocumulus

Name_____

A Warm Front

This illustration is a front between two air masses. A warm air mass is pushing a cold air mass.

Label the cloud types associated with the warm front.

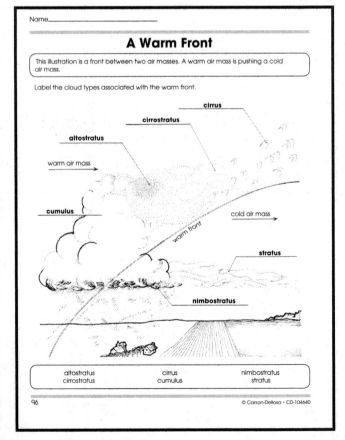

cirrus

cirrostratus

altostratus

warm air mass

cumulus   cold air mass

stratus

nimbostratus

altostratus	cirrus	nimbostratus
cirrostratus	cumulus	stratus

Answer Key

Name

Cloud Types

Label each cloud type shown.

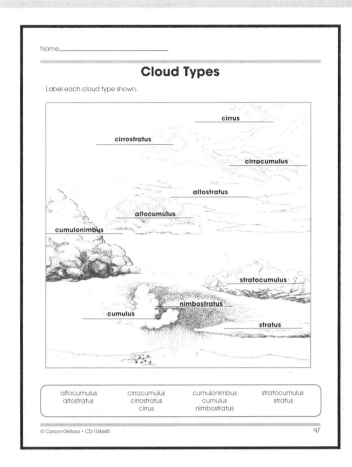

Name

Clouds and Weather

Different types of clouds are often associated with a specific kind of weather. Four different kinds of clouds are pictured. Write the name of the cloud type, a description of the cloud, and the kind of weather associated with each one.

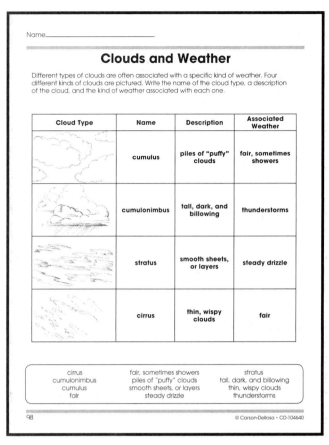

Cloud Type	Name	Description	Associated Weather
	cumulus	piles of "puffy" clouds	fair, sometimes showers
	cumulonimbus	tall, dark, and billowing	thunderstorms
	stratus	smooth sheets, or layers	steady drizzle
	cirrus	thin, wispy clouds	fair

cirrus
cumulonimbus
cumulus
fair

fair, sometimes showers
piles of "puffy" clouds
smooth sheets, or layers
steady drizzle

stratus
tall, dark, and billowing
thin, wispy clouds
thunderstorms

Name

Tomorrow's Weather Forecast

Check the accuracy of the weather forecasts in your area for the next week. Complete the chart by writing the forecast for tomorrow's weather and then recording the actual weather for that day. Indicate whether the forecast was accurate by circling *yes* or *no*.

Answers will vary.

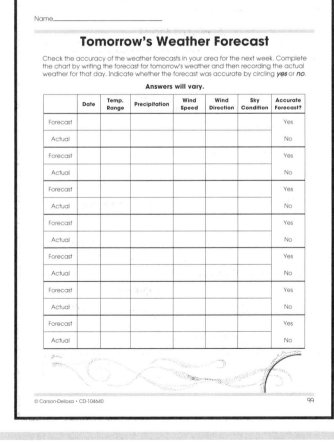

	Date	Temp. Range	Precipitation	Wind Speed	Wind Direction	Sky Condition	Accurate Forecast?
Forecast							Yes
Actual							No
Forecast							Yes
Actual							No
Forecast							Yes
Actual							No
Forecast							Yes
Actual							No
Forecast							Yes
Actual							No
Forecast							Yes
Actual							No
Forecast							Yes
Actual							No

Name

Weather Tools

Label each weather instrument.

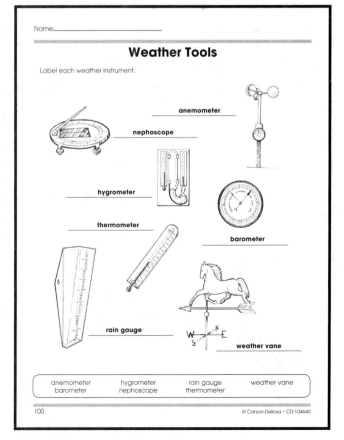

anemometer

nephoscope

hygrometer

thermometer

barometer

rain gauge

weather vane

anemometer   hygrometer   rain gauge   weather vane
barometer   nephoscope   thermometer

Answer Key

Name

Weather Instruments

Identify each instrument and tell what it measures.

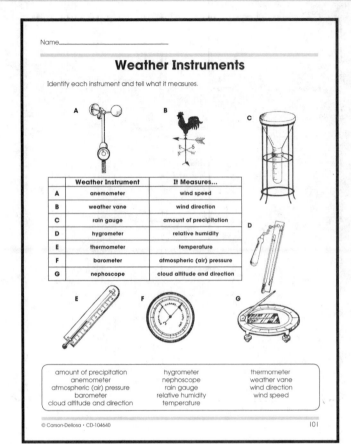

	Weather Instrument	It Measures...
A	anemometer	wind speed
B	weather vane	wind direction
C	rain gauge	amount of precipitation
D	hygrometer	relative humidity
E	thermometer	temperature
F	barometer	atmospheric (air) pressure
G	nephoscope	cloud altitude and direction

amount of precipitation	hygrometer	thermometer
anemometer	nephoscope	weather vane
atmospheric (air) pressure	rain gauge	wind direction
barometer	relative humidity	wind speed
cloud altitude and direction	temperature	

Weather Crossword

Use your knowledge of weather terms to complete the puzzle.

Across
3. Place where two air masses meet
5. Twisting funnel cloud
6. Rain that freezes as it falls
8. Scale used to measure wind speed
11. Measures air pressure
12. Measures wind speed
13. Sound made by rapidly heating and expanding air caused by lightning
14. Layered clouds

Down
1. Cloudy weather occurs in _____-pressure areas.
2. Soft, white crystalline flakes
3. A thick, ground-level mist
4. Measures temperature
7. Precipitation is measured with a rain _____.
9. Prediction of weather in the future
10. Calculates distance of clouds by echoing radio waves

anemometer	front	snow
barometer	gauge	stratus
Beaufort	low	thermometer
fog	radar	thunder
forecast	sleet	tornado